Option Trading Strategies

By

Bhushan Jadhav

"One of the funny things about the stock market is that every time one person buys, another sells, and both think they are astute".

All rights reserved
No part of this book may be reproduced in any form, by Photostat, Microfilm, xerography, or any other means or incorporated into Any information retrieval system, electronic or mechanical, Without the written permission of the copyright owner.

Option Trading strategies

By
Bhushan Jadhav

Copyright© Bhushan Jadhav 2018

Originally published in India

About the Author

Bhushan Jadhav is a young and enthusiastic author from Pune, Maharashtra. He holds Masters Degree in finance (MBA) and is certified as Market Professional by National Stock Exchange. After the success of his first book "Playing Stock Market with Technical Analysis", this is the next money making machine manufactured by him. Besides working for the India's finest financial institution, He is also a professional trader by religion.

Dedication

To My parents: Shri. Vijay Jadhav and Smt. Alka Jadhav
My Brother: Roshan Jadhav
My Happiness: Ziva Jadhav

Thank you for your love and support.

My Inspiration

My Grand Parents: Shri Kisan Rao Jadhav and Smt Ratnamala Jadhav

Chhatrapati Shivaji Maharaj,
&
Chhatrapati Sambhaji Maharaj.

Contents

1. Derivatives.
2. Types of Derivative Products.
3. Introduction to Options.
4. Options Terminology
5. Options Payoffs
   a) Payoff Profile of Buyer of Asset: Long Asset
   b) Payoff Profile for Seller of Asset: Short Asset
   c) Payoff Profile for Buyer of Call Options: Long Call
   d) Payoff Profile for Seller of Call Options: Short Call
   e) Payoff Profile for Buyer of Put Options: Long Put
   f) Payoff Profile for Seller of Put Options: Short Put
6. Option Strategy 1 : Long Call
7. Option Strategy 2 : Short Call
8. Option Strategy 3 : Synthetic Long Call
9. Option Strategy 4 : Long Put
10. Option Strategy 5 : Short Put
11. Option Strategy 6 : Covered Call
12. Option Strategy 7 : Long Combo
13. Option Strategy 8 : Protective Call / Synthetic Long Put
14. Option Strategy 9 : Covered Put
15. Option Strategy 10 : Long Straddle
16. Option Strategy 11 : Short Straddle
17. Option Strategy 12 : Long Strangle
18. Option Strategy 13 : Short Strangle
19. Option Strategy 14 : Collar
20. Option Strategy 15 : Bull Call Spread Strategy
21. Option Strategy 16 : Bull Put Spread Strategy
22. Option Strategy 17 : Bear Call Spread Strategy
23. Option Strategy 18 : Bear Put Spread Strategy
24. Option Strategy 19 : Long Call Butterfly
25. Option Strategy 20 : Short Call Butterfly
26. Option Strategy 21 : Long Call Condor
27. Option Strategy 22 : Short Call Condor
28. Option Greeks
    a) Delta
    b) Gamma
    c) Theta
    d) Vega
    e) Rho
    f) Lambda

Meaning of Derivative

Before we understand the true meaning of derivatives we must first know the old fashion definition of derivatives which is as follows-

Derivative is a product whose value is derived from the value of one or more basic variables, called underlying in a contractual manner. The underlying asset can be equity, index, foreign exchange, and commodity, an interest bearing security or any other asset.

If the price of the underlying asset increases or decreases then the price of the forward or future (derivative products) will also increase or decrease. So now the question is what is the need of the derivatives if the price of the derivative moves on the basis of underlying? Isn't that we can trade in underlying only?

The answer is derivative products initially emerged as hedging devices against fluctuations in commodity prices. For example, the price of the wheat is Rs.2000/quintal and a farmer wish to sell his crop at the current prices but the crop will take 3 more months to grow. The farmer feels that the price of the wheat is much volatile and fluctuates daily and the prices will not remain same after 3 months and it may fall to lower levels. So he decides to enter in to an agreement with the crop trader to sell his crop after 3 months at today's price (Rs.2000/quintal) and trader on the other hand thinks that the prices will increase as the supply will be short after some days. The farmer and the crop trader both enter in to an agreement to commit their promises at future date but at today's agreed price. Now after 3 months let's say the price of the wheat falls to Rs.1700/quintal. The farmer will now go to the crop trader and sell his crop for Rs. 2000/quintal, as he has locked the prices for himself and eliminates his risk against fluctuations in wheat price. The crop trader on the other side will lose Rs.300/quintal as he can buy it from the market at Rs.1700/quintal.

"The contract/agreement between farmer and the trader is a derivative."

The Chicago Board of Trade was set up in 1848 for the exchange trading of agricultural products such as wheat and corn. The Exchange put in place a mechanism that would play an important role in helping the agricultural community to plan for the future by enabling users of derivatives to lock in the prices they will receive for their goods before they were even ready for harvesting. In 1865 the Chicago Board formally established its General Rules. In 1870 the New York Cotton Exchange was established. Financial derivatives came into spotlight in the post-1970 period due to growing instability in the financial markets.

Types of Derivative Products

a) **Forwards** – A forward is a Private agreement between two parties – a buyer and a seller, to buy or sell an asset at a specific date in future at today's pre-agreed price. The buyer has the obligation to purchase an asset and the seller has obligation to sell an asset at a set price and at a specific date in future. A forward contract is a customized contract and is traded over the counter (OTC). As this is a private agreement between the two parties and is not traded on any exchanges, there is always a risk of counter party defaults.

b) **Futures**- A future contract is a standardized exchange-traded contract between two parties to buy or sell an asset at a certain time in future at a certain price. Future contract are special type of forward contracts and are traded on the exchange and eliminates counter party risk.

c) **Options**- An option is a contract written by a seller to buyer which gives the buyer the right but not the obligation to buy (in case of call option) or to sell (in case of put option) a particular asset, at a particular price (strike price/exercise price) in future. In return the seller collects a payment (the premium) from the buyer for granting the option. (We will see options in detail in next chapter).

d) **Warrants**- A warrant is similar to an Option. An option is an instrument of stock exchange whereas warrants are issued by a company. It gives the holder the right but not the obligation to buy an underlying security at a certain price, quantity and at a certain time in future from the issuing company. Warrants are one type of equity derivatives. The majority of the options traded on exchange have a maximum maturity of nine months whereas warrants have lives in years.

e) **LEAPS**- LEAPS means Long-Term Equity Anticipation Securities. LEAPS are similar to options, the long expiration date differentiate it from the short term options. LEAPS have a maturity of up to three years.

f) **Swaps**- Swaps are private agreements between parties to exchange cash flows of one party's financial instrument for those of the other party's financial instrument. Swaps are Over-the-counter contracts and are not traded on exchanges.

Example- "A" has Government Bonds of Rs.5 lakhs, yielding 10% per annum and "B" has corporate Bonds of Rs.5 lakhs, Yielding 11.5% per annum. B thinks that his corporate bonds may default and he wants safer investment vehicle. A on the other hand is not satisfied with the low coupon rates of Government bonds and wants higher yield from corporate bonds and can take the increased risk involved with corporate bonds. So they both enter in to an agreement with swap dealer by paying certain fees to swap dealer and now without changing the actual principal/notional amount or asset they will exchange the cash flows of others party's financial instrument i.e. coupon rates.

Introduction to Options

Options are contracts written by a seller to the buyer that gives the buyer the right but not the obligation to buy (in case of a call option) or to sell (in case of put option) a particular asset, at a particular price (strike price/exercise price) in future.

Example In case of future contract, the farmer and the trader decides to enter in to an agreement to buy or sell the crop at a certain time in future at a certain price. If the price of the crop in the market goes above the contracted price (price decided in contract) than the trader will gain by buying the crop from farmer at agreed price and selling it to market at higher prices. On the other side if the price drops down below contracted value in the market than the farmer will gain by selling it to trader at agreed price, as the contracted price is above the market price. Here both the parties have the obligation to fulfill their part of contract.

But in case of options, it gives the option to option buyer whether to execute the agreement or terminate it on a set date at a set price. Let say the farmer and the trader decides to execute the trade at Rs.2000/quintal and trader has bought the option contract from farmer i.e. The buyer of an option is the one who by paying the option premium buys the right but not the obligation to exercise his option on the seller/writer of the contract. Now trader has the option to execute the agreement or terminate it on a set date at a set price i.e. he has the right to buy the crop from farmer on a set date at a set price but he does not have the obligation to do so. If the prices in the market go above the contract price he can exercise his right on farmer and can buy the crop at agreed prices. He will call the farmer to fulfill the obligation and buys the crop from him. **This option is called as Call Option.**

But in case if the prices in the market drops below contract price than the trader will exist from the contract because he can buy it at lower prices from market. To obtain this right, option buyer (Trader in this case) has to pay a premium amount to option seller (Farmer). It is just like giving a token amount to writer/seller (Farmer) of the contract and in return buying the right to execute the agreement. But in case if he does not want to execute the agreement he has to leave his option premium (Token amount) and this premium will be the loss of option buyer (Trader) and gain of option seller/writer (Farmer). This premium is the motive which option seller wants to gain by writing the contract to the buyer and giving the right to option buyer.

An example of put option A farmer wants to sell his crop to trader at some certain price and date, let say 2500/quintal. Now farmer can buy the put option from trader which gives him the right to sell his crop at 2500/quintal to trader at certain time in future but he does not have any obligation to do so i.e. if price of the crop rises to 3000/quintal in market than the farmer can exist from the contract and leave his token amount (amount paid to buy put) and sell his crop at market at higher prices. But in case if the prices of the crops drops down to 2000 levels than he has a right to sell or put his crop to buyer at 2500/quintal and the trader (Option seller) has the obligation to buy it from the farmer because he has already taken the token amount (option premium) from the farmer. **This option is called as put option.**

OPTIONS TERMINOLOGY

Index options These options have the index as the underlying asset. In India, they have European style settlement i.e. they can be exercised only on the expiration date itself. Ex. Nifty options (Nifty is an Indian Index).

Stock options Stock options are options on individual stocks. A stock option contract gives the holder the right to buy or sell the underlying shares at the specified price and specified time. They have European style settlement.

Buyer of an option The buyer of an option is the one who by paying the option premium buys the right but not the obligation to exercise his option on the seller/writer.

Writer / seller of an option The writer / seller of a call/put option are the one who receives the option premium and is thereby obliged to sell/buy the asset if the buyer exercises on him.

Call option A call option gives the holder the right but not the obligation to buy an asset by a certain date for a certain price.

Put option A put option gives the holder the right but not the obligation to sell an asset by a certain date for a certain price.

Option price/premium Option price is the price which the option buyer pays to the option seller to buy the right. It is also referred to as the option premium.

Expiration date The date specified in the options contract is known as the expiration date, the exercise date, the strike date or the maturity. This is the last day of the contract to exercise the right, after this the contract becomes void.

Strike price The price specified in the options contract is known as the strike price or the exercise price. This is the agreed price to exchange the assets.

Spot price The spot price means the price of the underlying asset. This is the actual/real price of the asset.

American options American options are options that can be exercised at any time up to the expiration date.

European options European options are options that can be exercised only on the expiration date itself.

In the money options An in-the-money (ITM) option is an option that would lead to a positive cash flow to the holder if it were exercised immediately. A call option on the index is said to be in-the-money when the current index level (spot price) is higher than the strike price (i.e. spot price > strike price). If the index is much higher than the strike price, the call is said to be deep ITM. In the case of a put, the put is ITM if the index is below the strike price (spot price < strike price).

Suppose the spot price (current index level) of Nifty is 8000 then all the Call options with strike price below 8000 are in the money (ITM) call options. Let say 7900, 7800, 7700 are in the money call options whereas call options with strike price of 7600, 7500 and 7400 are deep in the money call options. Here spot price is higher than strike price (i.e. 8000>7900). If you exercised the 7900 call option when nifty is at 8000, you will gain (Rs.100 – Premium paid for buying the options). If you exercised the 7800 call option when nifty is at 8000 you will gain (Rs.200 – Premium paid for buying the options) and vice versa. Your gain is the difference between the spot price and strike price minus the premium paid for buying the options.

For in the money (ITM) put options the spot price of nifty is lower than the strike price (i.e. spot price<strike price). If nifty is trading at 8000 levels than all the put options with

strike price above 8000 are in the money put options. Ex. 8100, 8200, 8300 are in the money put options whereas put options with strike price of 8500, 8600 and 8700 are called as deep in the money put options.

In the money options generates positive cash flow to the holder if it were exercised immediately.

In simple, in-the money options means buyer of the options has advantage over the seller of the option i.e. the rate at which the call option buyer has agreed to buy the asset from seller is lower than the market price of the asset and generates a positive cash flow for option buyer, as he is buying at lower price from seller than that of market. Similarly, for put option the rate agreed by the put option buyer to sell the asset is higher than the market price of the asset which gives him advantage to sell his asset at higher prices than market price.

At-the-money option At-the-money (ATM) option is an option that would lead to zero cash flow if it were exercised immediately. An option on the index is at-the-money when the current index is equal to the strike price (i.e. spot price = strike price).

Out-of-the-money option Out-of-the-money (OTM) option is an option that would lead to a negative cash flow if it were exercised immediately. A call option on the index is out-of-the-money when the current index stands at a level which is less than the strike price (i.e. spot price < strike price). If the index is much lower than the strike price, the call is said to be deep OTM. In the case of a put, the put is OTM if the index is above the strike price.

Intrinsic value of an option The option premium has two elements, intrinsic value and the time value. The intrinsic value is the difference between the underlying price and the strike price.

Option Premium= Intrinsic value + Time value

Intrinsic Value of call options = Underlying price – Strike price

Intrinsic value of put options = Strike Price – Underlying Price

In the money options have the intrinsic value i.e. strike price is less than underlying price for call options and strike price is above the underlying price for put options.

In the money Call options=Strike price < Underlying price

In the money Put options= Strike price > Underlying price

Intrinsic value of Out of the money (OTM) options is Zero.

Time value of an option The difference between the options premium and its intrinsic value is called as time value of options.

Time value of options= Options Premium – Intrinsic value

The premium which is in excess of options intrinsic value is referred as time value of options. Options which are out of the money or at the money have only time value. At the money options have maximum time value. At expiration options have no time value. The longer the time to expiry, the greater is the option time value.

Now the question is why the time value exits? It is when the option buyer and seller enters in to a contract to exchange the asset at a certain future date at certain price, the option buyer has more advantage over option seller because the time to expire the contract is long and there is a high possibility of price fluctuations in underlying asset and option seller is exposed to this volatile price risk which option buyer has already fixed it with option seller but here option seller has a risk of unlimited loss due to price fluctuation till the time of contract expiration. Due to this time period, the options seller charges a higher premium from option buyer to compensate him with the risk associated with the option selling. **It's like a compensation given by option buyer to option seller for allowing more time to guess the movements of the market.**

Options Payoffs

Option traders use the profit and loss payoffs diagrams to evaluate how the strategy is performing over a range of prices. It also helps traders to evaluate the risk and reward of the position, at a glance. Traders can actually visualize their positions by drawing these payoffs diagrams. Now let us see how to draw these options payoffs diagrams.

The values are plotted along X and Y axes. The horizontal axis (X-axis) shows the price of the underlying; the prices are low at the left and rises towards the right. The current underlying price is centered on X-axis. The vertical axis (Y-axis) represents the profit and loss of the position. The breakeven point indicating no profit and no loss is usually centered on Y-axis. Profits are shown above this centered point and losses are shown below this point.

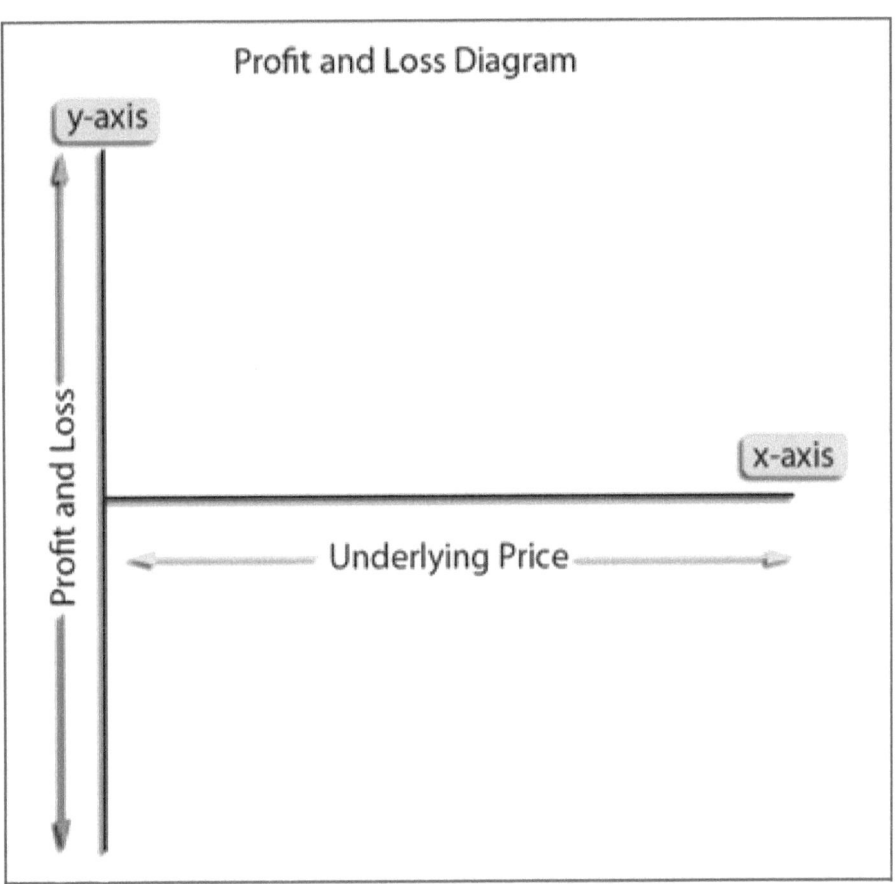

Payoff profile of buyer of asset: Long asset

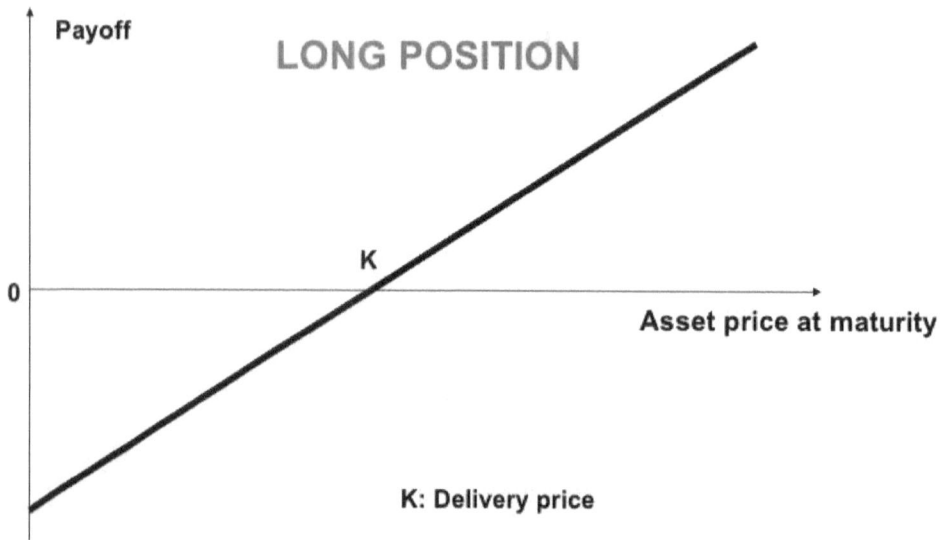

When investor purchases the asset it is said to be "long" the asset. If the stock price goes up the payoff line goes above the zero line sloping slightly towards right side to the extent the stock raises (makes profit). Here the current stock price is denoted by "K".

Pay off profile of investor who went long on Nifty at 5700

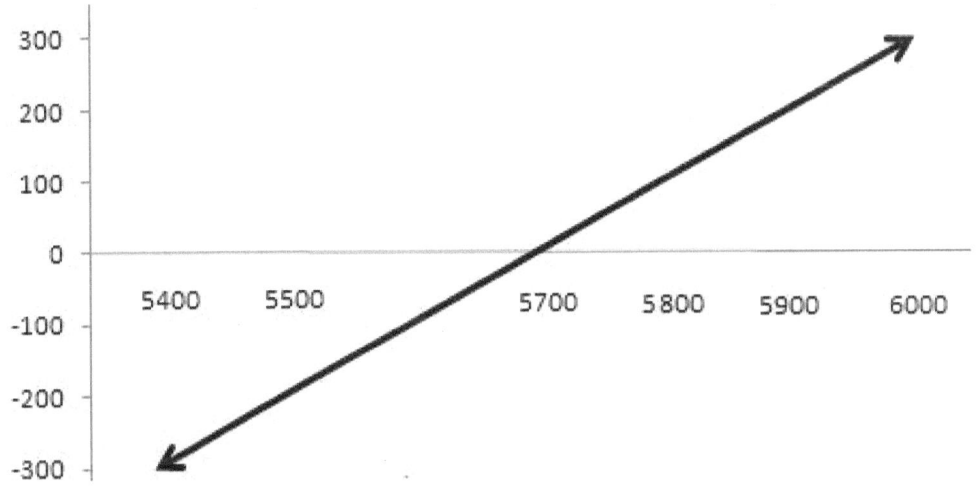

The figure shows that the investor went long on nifty at 5700. If nifty goes up, he profits. If nifty falls he losses. +300 and -300 shows his profits and losses if nifty touches to 6000 or 5400 level. The prices are rising on right side and declining on left side on X-axis. The profit and loss is shown on Y-axis.

Payoff profile for seller of asset: Short asset

When investor sells the asset it is said to be "Short" the asset. If the stock price goes up the payoff line goes below the zero line towards right side to the extent the stock raises (incurring losses). As the investor has sold the asset he will gain when the asset price starts to fall.

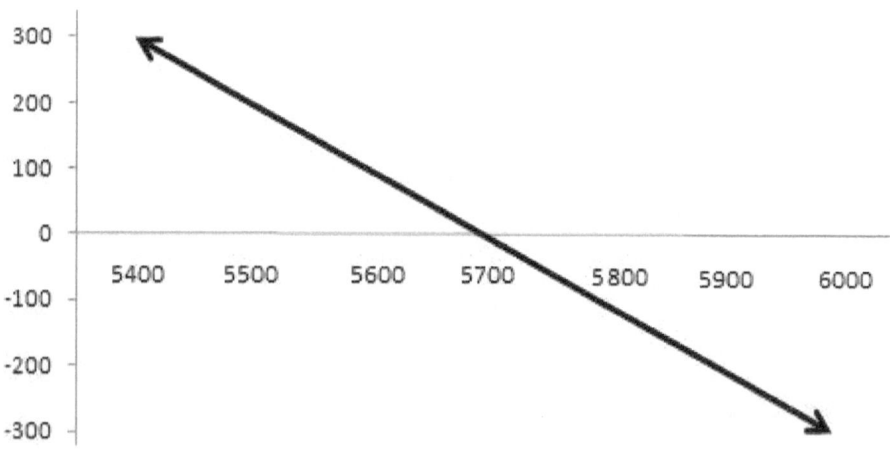

Suppose investor sold the nifty at 5700. Now he will gain when nifty falls below 5700 and the payoff graph will looks like the above figure. The figure shows that the line has reached to +300 on left side means nifty is trading at 5400 below 300 points from selling point of 5700. If graph shows –300 than it means nifty has risen to 6000 levels. This is how a short asset payoff profile will look like on the graph.

Payoff profile for buyer of call options: Long Call

Buyer of a call option means he has the right to buy the underlying asset at the strike price specified in the option contract. The buyer's profit is totally depends on the spot price of the underlying asset. If the spot price of the underlying asset on expiry is more than the strike price of option than the buyer makes the profit. Higher the spot price more is the profit. Here spot price is more than the strike price which means buyer has the right to buy the asset at the strike price of option. If the spot price of the underlying is less than the strike price than the buyer will let his option expire as he can buy the asset from market at lower price than strike price. Here he will lose the premium he has paid to buy the option thus his losses is limited to the extent of premium paid.

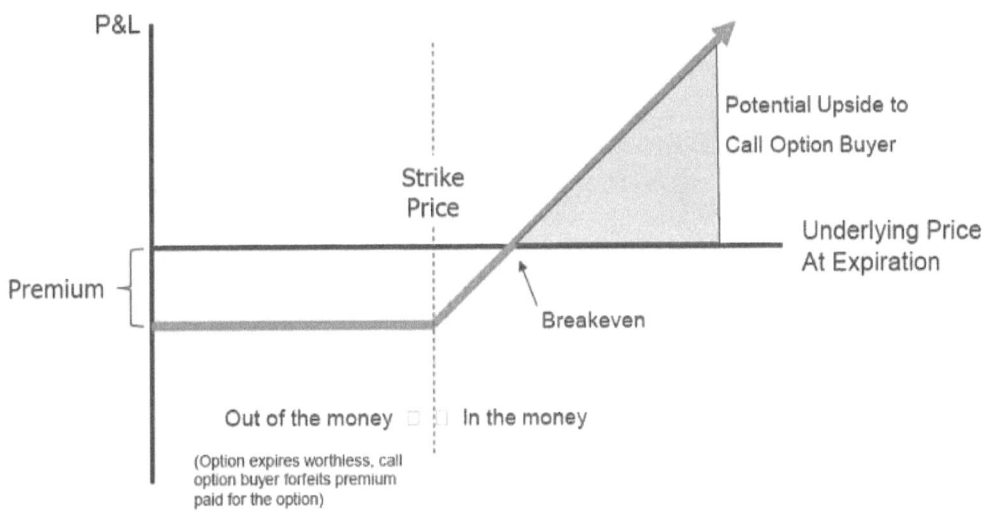

Example- If a buyer has bought the nifty 6000 call option @ Rs.100, Here the strike price is 6000 and the premium paid for buying the option is Rs.100 which means he has bought the right to buy the nifty @6000 on expiry date. Now if nifty rises above 6100 which is his breakeven because he has paid the premium of Rs.100, he will start earning profit to the extent the nifty rises above 6100. On expiry if nifty closes at 6300 than he will exercise the option and his profit will be Rs. 200 (intrinsic value of call option i.e. 300 - Premium paid i.e. 100). In this case his potential upside is unlimited as the nifty can rise to any level but if nifty falls below 6000 level than his loss is limited to the extent the premium is paid i.e.Rs.100. The buyer of call option will let his option expire if nifty closes below the strike price of the option i.e. below 6000 level.

See payoff profile of buyer of Nifty Call option.

Strike Price=5000, premium Paid= Rs.200, Breakeven=5200, profit= Rs.300 if nifty closes at 5500.

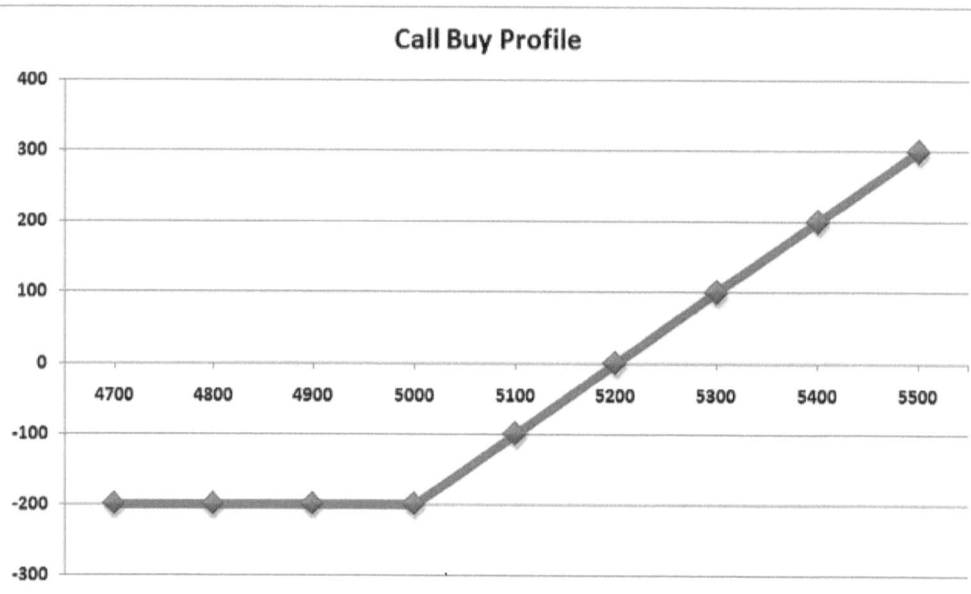

Here loss is limited to Rs.200 but profit is unlimited to the extent the nifty raises.

Payoff profile for writer (seller) of call options: Short Call

Seller of call option will charge a premium for selling the option or giving the right to buyer of the option to buy the underlying at strike price of the option. Thus, whatever is the buyers profit is the seller's loss. On expiry if the spot price of the asset exceeds the strike price of call option the buyer will exercise his right on option seller. Hence as the spot price increases the writer/seller of the call option start making losses. The risk which is associated with selling the call option and providing more time to buyer of the call option to let his option price moves in his favor is compensated by charging a premium on option buyer by option seller. This premium is the motivational factor which attracts traders to write or sell the option. If on expiry if the asset price stays below the strike price of the call option, the option buyer will let his option expire/un-exercised and this will be the profit of the option seller.

Strike Price=5000, premium received= Rs.200, Breakeven=5200, Maximum profit= Rs.200 if nifty closes at or below 5000 level. Loss= loss starts above 5200 level to the extent nifty rises till expiry.

See payoff profile of seller of Nifty Call option.

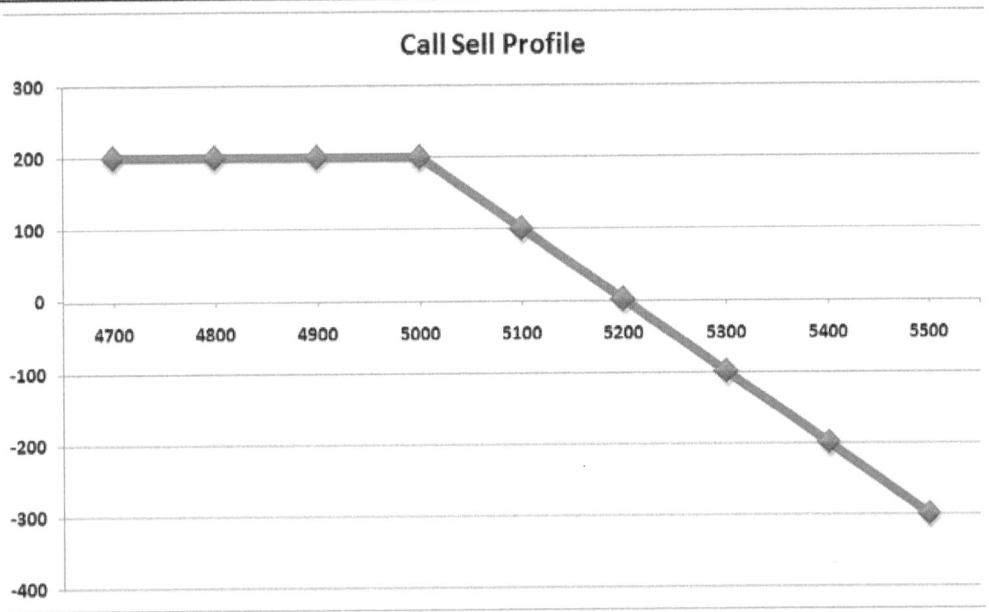

In above diagram the seller has sold the call option of strike price of 5000 at Rs.200, which means the buyer has paid Rs.200 to seller to buy the call option. Here Rs.200 is credited to seller's account which means 5200 is the breakeven point for seller of the options because at this point the intrinsic value of the call option will be Rs.200 (spot 5200- strike5000) and if the buyer of the option exercises his right the seller will have to provide him nifty @5000 (strike price) by purchasing it from market at 5200 (spot price) and selling him at 5000 thus making a loss of Rs.200 but for this he has charged the premium of Rs.200. Here the seller of a call option is at no profit-no loss situation but as the nifty rises above 5200 his position starts making the losses. If nifty reaches to 5500 level the intrinsic value of call option on expiry will be Rs.500, making a loss of Rs.300 to option seller and a profit of Rs.300 to option buyer.

Payoff profile for buyer of put options: Long put

A put option gives the buyer the right to sell the underlying asset at the strike price specified in the option contract. Let say the trader buys the put option of nifty of strike price of 6000, which means he can sell the nifty at 6000 to seller of the put option. The put option buyer has a right to sell the nifty to put option seller at the strike price and the put option seller has the obligation to buy the nifty from put option buyer if he exercises his right on the expiry.

The profit/loss that the buyer makes on the option depends on the spot price of the underlying. If upon expiration, the spot price is below the strike price, he makes a profit. Lower the spot price more is the profit he makes. If the spot price of the underlying is higher than the strike price, he lets his option expire un-exercised. His loss in this case is the premium he paid for buying the option.

If the spot price is below the strike price than option seller can sell the underlying asset at strike price. But if the underlying asset is above the strike price he can sell the nifty at market at higher prices letting his option expire.

The profit is unlimited to the put option buyer to the extent the underlying asset falls but his loss is limited to the premium he has paid for acquiring his right to sell the underlying asset at strike price.

See payoff profile of buyer of Nifty put option.

Strike Price=5100, premium paid= Rs.100, Breakeven=5000, Maximum loss= Rs.100 if nifty closes at or above 5100 level. If nifty closes at 4700 level on expiry than the gain will be Rs.300 i.e. Strike price – Spot price (5100-4700=400 less premium paid Rs.100).

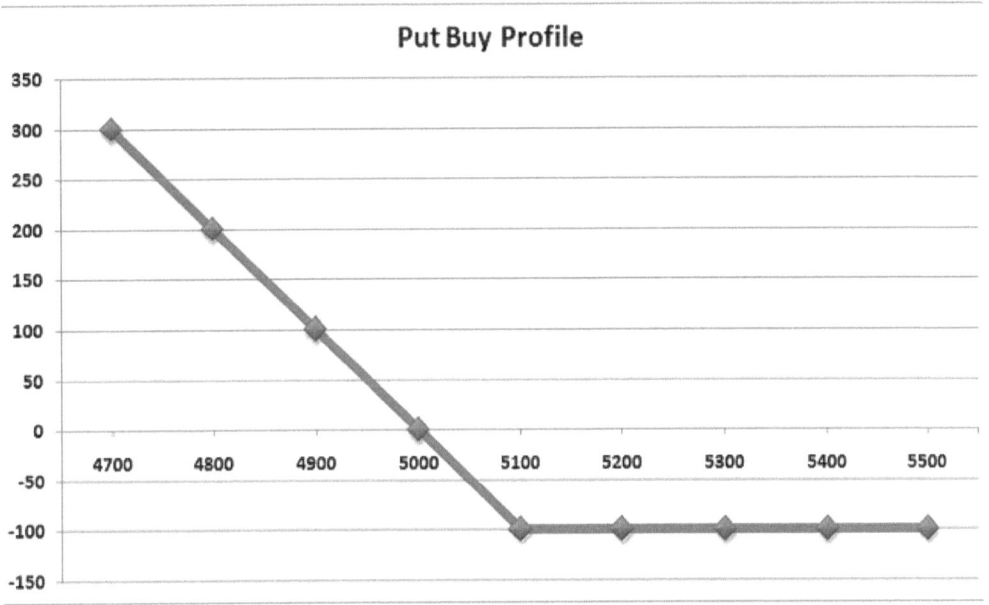

Payoff profile for writer (seller) of put options: Short put

Seller of put option will charge a premium for selling the option or giving the right to buyer of the option to sell the underlying asset at strike price of the option. The profit/loss that the buyer makes on the option depends on the spot price of the underlying. Whatever is the buyer's profit is the seller's loss. If upon expiration, the spot price happens to be below the strike price, the buyer will exercise the option on the writer. If upon expiration the spot price of the underlying is more than the strike price, the buyer lets his option un-exercised and the writer gets to keep the premium.

See payoff profile of seller of Nifty put option.

Strike Price=5100, premium received= Rs.100, Breakeven=5000, Maximum profit= Rs.100 if nifty closes at or above 5100 level. Loss= loss starts below 5000 level to the extent nifty drops down till expiry.
In below figure if nifty expires at 4700 level than the loss will be Rs.300 (5100-4700-premium received) i.e. Strike price –Spot price-premium received.

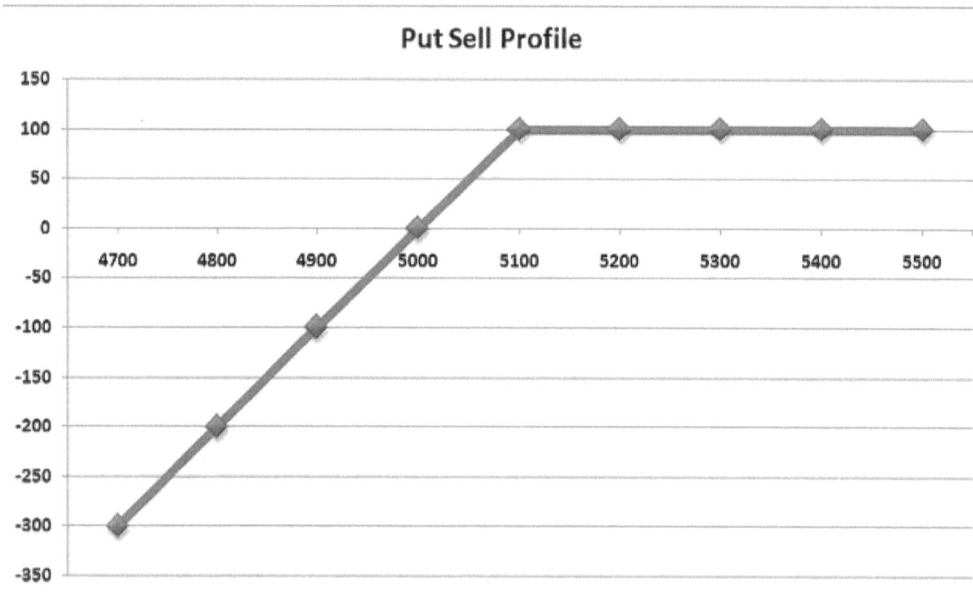

STRATEGY 1- LONG CALL

Long call or buying a call is a very basic option strategy. The strategy is suitable for the investors who are very bullish on a particular stock or index. When you buy a call means you expect the stock or index to rise. By buying a call of a particular strike price means, buyer has a right to buy the underlying asset at the strike price of the option without any obligation i.e. if the underlying asset price remains below the strike price of the option he will let his option expire.

This long call strategy is an excellent way to capture the upside movement of underlying asset with limited downside risk.

Example- Mr. Roshan is a new investor who is familiar with buying & selling of stocks and now wants to trade with options. He is very bullish on State Bank of India but instead of investing a huge capital on buying a stock which is worth Rs.200 per share, he prefers to invest with limited risk and nominal capital. When the stock is at Rs. 200 on 5th Jan, he buys the call option with a strike price of Rs.220 at a premium of Rs.3, expiring on 28th Jan. If the stock goes above Rs. 223, Mr. Roshan will make a net profit to the extent stock rises after deducting the premium on expiry day. Let say the stock is trading at Rs.230 on 28th Jan (Expiry day), the intrinsic value of call will be Rs.10 (Spot price –Strike price). Here Mr. Roshan will gain Rs.7 as he has paid Rs. 3 as a premium for buying the option.

Breakeven= Strike Price + Premium

= Rs.220+Rs.3

=Rs223

Let say lot size of one SBI call option is 1000qty, which means you have to buy in multiples of 1000. It gives the right to buy 1000 SBI stock at the strike price of the option.

Mr. Roshan's profit will be = Spot price − Strike price i.e. 230−220=Rs.10 less premium paid of Rs.3 (Rs.10 − Rs.3 = Rs.7).

Total Net profit= 7*1000= Rs.7000.

In case the stock stays at or below Rs.220, he can let his option expire worthless with a maximum loss of premium (Rs.3 * 1000=Rs.3000).

When to use Long call strategy

Investor is very bullish on the underlying.

Risk & Reward associated with this strategy

Here the loss is limited to the extent of premium paid but profit is unlimited as stock can rise to any level. Reward is unlimited.

Breakeven

Strike Price + Premium

Strategy- Long call option

	Spot Price	200
Call Option	Strike Price	220
Mr. Roshan Pays	Premium	3
	Break Even Point (Strike Price + Premium)	223

The Payoff Schedule

On Expiry Stock Closes at	Net Payoff from call option
160	-3
170	-3
180	-3
200	-3
210	-3
223	0
230	7
240	17

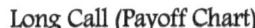

Long Call (Payoff Chart)

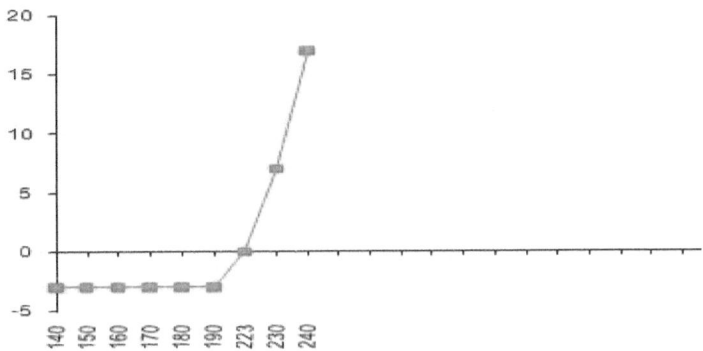

STRATEGY 2 – SHORT CALL

When you buy a call you expect the underlying asset to rise. While selling or shorting the call means you expect the underlying to fall. When an investor is very bearish on underlying asset he can sell the call options. Shorting a call is opposite of buying a call. Call option seller has the obligation to deliver the asset to buyer of an option on exercising his right on expiry. If the underlying asset stays below the strike price of the option the option buyer will let his option expire worthless and this is where the option seller makes his gain. He retains the entire premium paid by option buyer. Here the profit is limited to option premium but the losses can be unlimited as the option price can rise to any extent.

The strategy is suitable to the investors who are aggressive and are very bearish on the underlying asset. The strategy is risky as the option seller is exposed to unlimited risk.

Example-Mr. Amitabh Bacchan is very bearish on the Nifty and expects it to fall. He sells the call option with a strike price of 6000 at a premium of Rs.250 when nifty is at 6200. If nifty stays at 6000 or below, the call option buyer will not exercise his right and Mr. Amitabh Bacchan can retain the entire premium of Rs.250.

When to use short call strategy

Investor is very bearish on the underlying asset and can take the risk of selling options.

Risk & Reward associated with this strategy

The risk is unlimited to the extent the underlying rises. The reward is limited to the option premium received.

Breakeven

Strike Price + Premium (* Breakeven Point is from the view point of Call Option Buyer)

Strategy: Short call option

	Spot Price	6200
Call Option	Strike Price	6000
Mr. Amitabh Receives	Premium	250
	Break Even Point (Strike Price + Premium)	6250

The Payoff Schedule

On Expiry Nifty Closes at	Net Payoff from call option
5600	250
5700	250
5800	250
5900	250
6000	250
6100	150
6200	50
6250	0
6300	-50
6400	-150
6500	-250
6600	-350

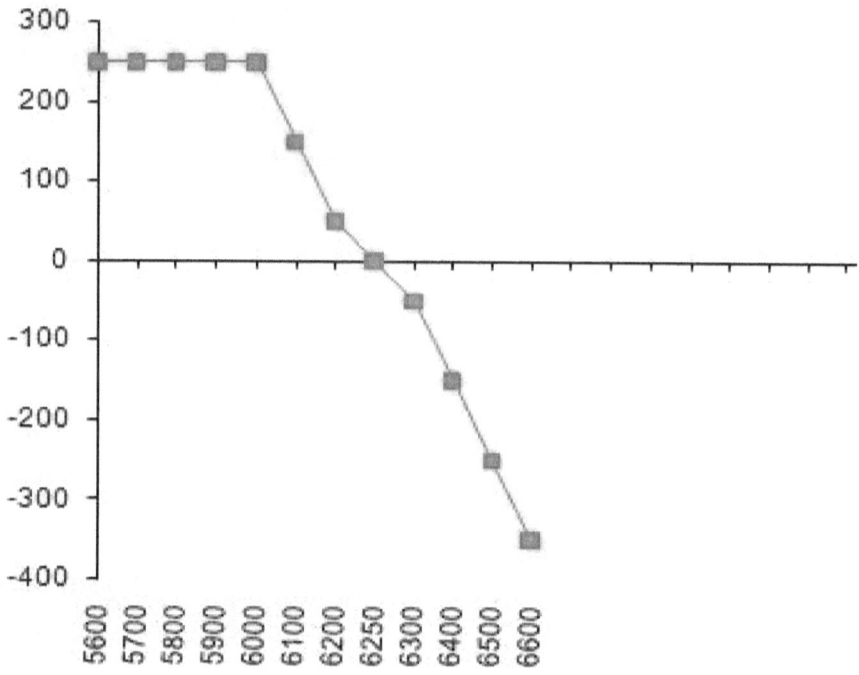

This strategy is also called as naked call because the investor do not holds the underlying stock that he is shorting.

STRATEGY 3 – SYNTHETIC LONG CALL – BUY STOCK, BUY PUT

The strategy is like buying insurance for the stocks you own. An investor buys a stock in anticipation that it will rise in future but what if the price of the stock went down. Buying a put on the stock insures against the fall in price of the stocks. Put gives the right to sell the stock at the strike price specified in the contract. If you buy the put at the strike price which is equal to purchase price of the stock it means you have bought (ATM) at the money strike price option, if you buy the put slightly below the stock price it means you have bought (OTM) out of the money put options. For (ITM) in the money put options you have to buy put with a strike price which is higher than the stock price.

Buying put insures you from falling prices of the stocks. When the stock price starts to fall, put option insures you that you have the right to sell your stocks at the strike price specified in the contract. No matter how much your stock falls but if you have bought the put means you can sell your stock at the strike price of the put.

The strategy is bullish though you have not bought the call option but you have bought the put option which insures you against the adverse movement of the stock. This is why it is also called Synthetic Long call.

If the price of the stock rises investor can benefit of the price rise but if it falls he can exercise the put option. The put option stops the further losses. The strategy has limited loss and unlimited profit (from the stock price rise) after subtracting the put premium.

Example- Mr. Ranveer is bullish on Nestle Ltd stock. He buys the stock at Rs.6000 on 4th March. To protect against the fall in prices of stock Mr. Ranveer buys an insurance i.e. put option with a strike price of Rs. 5900 (OTM) by paying a premium of Rs. 100 expiring on 31st March.

Now the breakeven for Mr. Ranveer is Rs.6100 (Stock Price + Premium). If stock starts to move further Rs.6100 Mr. Ranveer can make unlimited profit to the extent the stock rises by letting his put option expire worthless. But if the stock price starts to fall and if it finally ended at Rs.5500 on expiry day, he will lose Rs.500 per share on the stock but the intrinsic value of the 5900 put option will be Rs.400 thus making a profit of Rs.300 after deducting the premium Rs.100. So in overall he will lose 500-300=Rs.200 (loss on stock – profit on put option). This is how the put option capped your losses and stops you from further losses. If the stock falls to 5000 level than also he will lose Rs. 200 i.e. Rs.1000 on stock and profit on put option will be Rs.800 (Intrinsic value of put option Rs.900- Premium paid Rs.100).

When to use Synthetic Long call strategy

When the investor is conservatively bullish on a particular stock or index he can use this strategy. When investor is concerned about the near term downside risk but his long term perspective on stock is good.

Risk & Reward associated with this strategy

This is a low risk strategy. The loss is limited to the Stock price + Put Premium – Put Strike Price. The reward from the strategy is potentially unlimited.

Breakeven

Stock Price + Put option premium

(* Breakeven is from the view point of Mr. Ranveer. He has to recover the cost of the Put Option purchase price + the stock price to break even.)

Strategy: Synthetic Long call: But Stock + Buy Put option

Buy Stock (Mr. Ranveer pays)	Current price of the Nestle Ltd. Stock	6000
Put Option	Strike Price	5900
Mr. Ranveer Pays for buying put option	Premium	100
	Breakeven (Stock price + Put option premium)	6100

The Payoff Schedule

Nestle Ltd. Closes at (Rs.) on expiry	Payoff from the stock (Rs.)	Net payoff from the put option (Rs.) (Intrinsic value– premium paid)	Net payoff (Rs.)
5400	–600	400 (500-100)	–200
5500	–500	300 (400-300)	–200
5600	–400	200 (300-200)	–200
5700	–300	100 (200-100)	–200
5800	–200	0 (100-100)	–200
5900	–100	–100 (0-100)	–200
6000	0	–100 (0-100)	–100
6100	100	–100 (0-100)	0
6200	200	–100 (0-100)	100
6300	300	–100 (0-100)	200
6400	400	–100 (0-100)	300
6500	500	–100 (0-100)	400

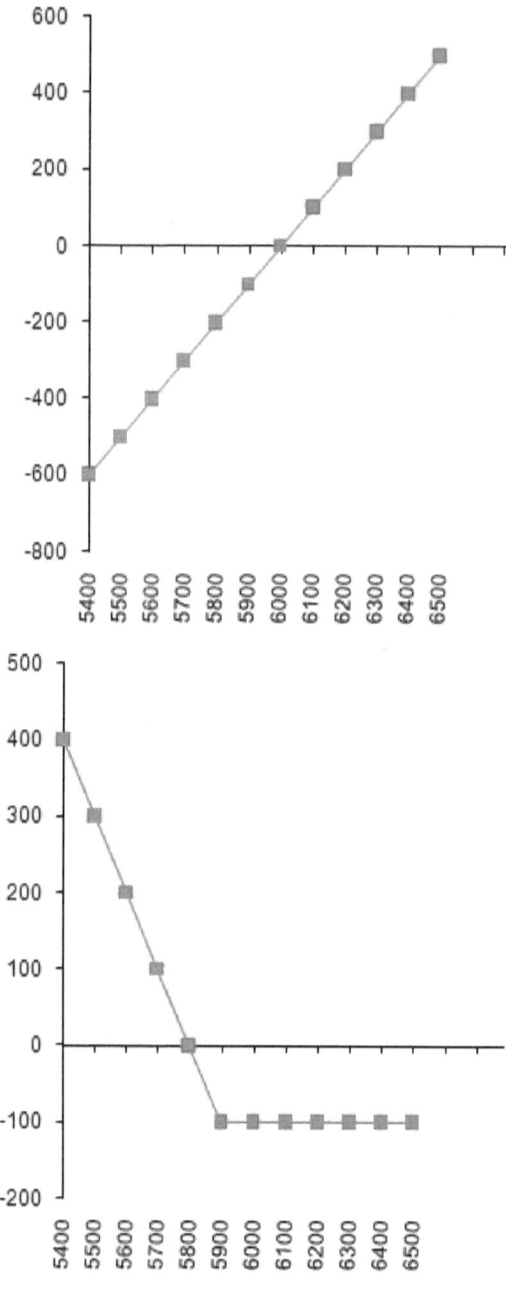

Buy Stock + Buy Put = Synthetic Call

Synthetic Long Call (Payoff chart)

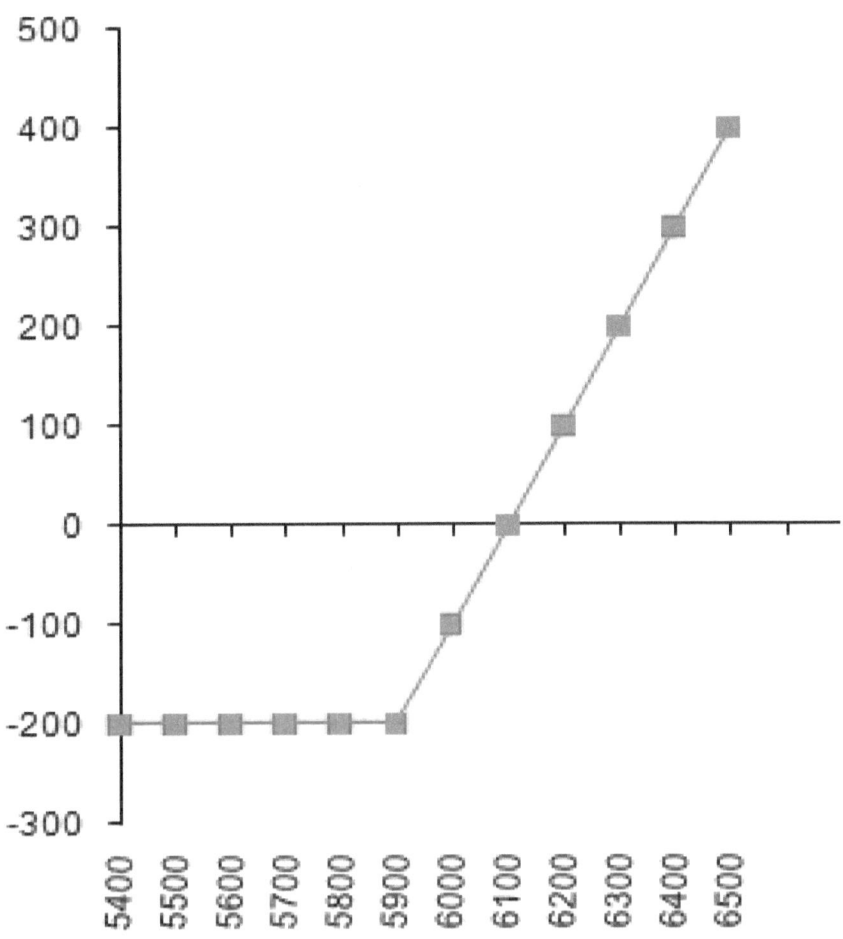

The strategy aims at protecting any downside risk in near term.

STRATEGY 4 – LONG PUT

Long put or buying a put means you are very bearish on the stock or index. When an investor is bearish on a particular stock or index, he can buy the put option which gives him the right to sell the stock at pre-specified price. The put option gives him the right to sell the stock at the strike price. Put option buyer can take the advantage of a falling market.

Example- Mr. Nawazuddin is very bearish on nifty on 1st Oct, when nifty is at 7000. He buys a put option with a strike price of 6800 at a premium of Rs.120, expiring on 30th Oct. If the nifty goes below 6680 (6800-120), Mr. Nawazuddin will make profit on exercising the option. In case if the nifty rise or stays above 6800 he will let his option expire worthless with a maximum loss of the premium paid by him.

When to use Long Put strategy

When investor is very bearish on a particular stock or index and he wants to take the advantage of falling market, he can buy the put option.

Risk & Reward associated with this strategy

The risk is limited to the amount of premium paid by an investor to buy the put option. The rewards are unlimited to the extent the index or stock falls.

Breakeven

Strike Price – Premium paid

Strategy: Buy Put option

	Current Nifty Index	7000
Put Option	Strike Price	6800
Mr. Nawazuddin Pays for buying put option	Premium	120
	Breakeven (Strike price - Put option premium)	6680

The Payoff Schedule

On Expiry Nifty Closes at	Net Payoff from call option
6100	580
6200	480
6300	380
6400	280
6500	180
6600	80
6680	0
6800	-120
6900	-120
7000	-120
7100	-120
7200	-120
7300	-120
7400	-120
7500	-120

Long Put (Payoff chart)

STRATEGY 5 – SHORT PUT

Short put is opposite of buying a put. Shorting a put means investor is bullish on the stock/index or at minimum he expects it to remain sideways. By selling put you earn a premium against which you give someone the right to sell the stock at a strike price. If the stock price increases beyond the strike price, short put position will make profit by the amount of premium received because the put option buyer will not exercise his right on the seller as he can sell the underlying at the market price (which is higher than strike price). But in case if the stock price falls below the strike price of the option the option buyer will exercise his right on option seller (option buyer can sell the underlying at strike price which is higher than the market price).

Example- Mr. Sharukh is bullish on nifty when it is trading at 7550. He sells the put option with a strike price of Rs.7500 at a premium of Rs.80 expiring on 31st March. If the nifty stays above 7500 Mr. Sharukh will gain the amount of premium as the put buyer won't exercise his right and the price of put will become zero (No intrinsic value). In case if nifty falls below Rs.7420 (Break even) Mr. Sharukh will start making loss to the extent the nifty falls below 7420.

When to use Long Put strategy

When investor is very bullish on the stock and wants to take the advantage of time decay (time value of options).

Risk & Reward associated with this strategy

The put seller has limited profit to the extent the premium is received. The potential losses can be unlimited as the stock or index can fall to any level.

Breakeven

Put Strike Price – Premium received

Strategy: Sell Put option

	Current Nifty Index	7550
Put Option	Strike Price	7500
Mr. Sharukh receives	Premium	80
	Breakeven (Strike price − Put option premium)	7420

* Breakeven Point is from the point of Put Option Buyer.

The Payoff Schedule

On Expiry Nifty Closes at	Net Payoff from call option
7000	−500
7100	−400
7200	−300
7300	−200
7400	−100
7420	0
7500	80
7600	80
7700	80
7800	80
7900	80
8000	80

Short Put (Payoff chart)

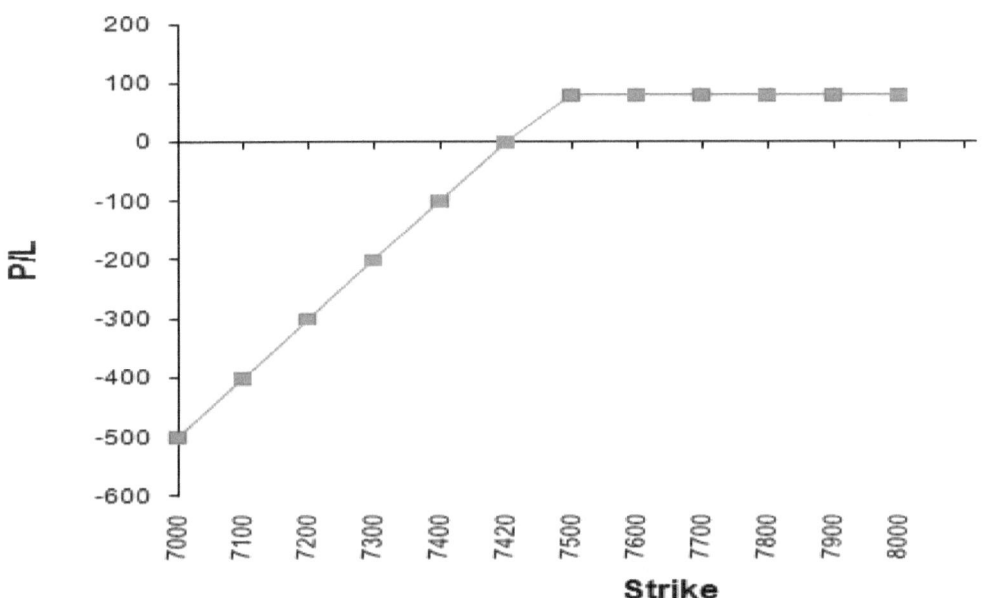

STRATEGY 6 – COVERED CALL

The strategy is suitable for the investor who owns the stock of a particular company and he is neutral to moderately bullish about the stock. Though the investor has bought the stock in anticipation that the long term prospects for the stock is good but he finds that in near term it will not raise much and may remain sideways. So now what the best he can do here with the stock is, he can sell the call option on a stock he already owns. This strategy of selling call on the stock which investor already owns is called as covered call. The call option which is sold usually is OTM call. The call will not get exercised unless the stock price increases above the strike price. Selling call provides an income to the seller in the form of premium received from option buyer.

When an investor sells a call means he has provided the right to the option buyer to buy the underlying asset at the strike price specified in the contract. If the stock price do not increase above the strike price the call option buyer will not exercise his right on the seller as he can buy the stock from market at the lower price (less than the strike price). Here the option seller will retain the premium with him which is an extra income on the stock he already owns. But incase if the stock prices increases above the strike price, the investor will not mind existing the stock at a certain price (target price). An investor can sell the call option at the strike price at which he would be comfortable to exit the stock. The call option buyer will exercise his right when stock increases above strike price because now it's profitable to option buyer to buy the underlying asset at the strike price which is lower than the market price.

So by selling call option an investor can earn additional income as a premium on the stocks he already owns and whose view on the stock is neutral to moderately bullish. This is why the strategy is called as a Covered Call strategy because the Call sold is backed by a stock owned by the Call Seller (investor). The income gets capped after the stock reaches the strike price.

Example- Mr. Salman has bought Bajaj Auto stock for Rs.2500 and sold call option of strike price of Rs.2700 for Rs. 40. It means Mr. Salman thinks that the stock will not rise above Rs.2700 and if it does he is comfortable to exit the stock at the targeted price. Mr. Salman will receive a premium of Rs.40 for selling the call which will be retain by him if the stock do not increases above Rs.2700. By doing this he reduces the cost of buying the stock by Rs.40 (Rs.2500-Rs.40 premium received).

Call option buyer will exercise his right only when the stock crosses the strike price + premium paid by him. He can get the stock at the strike price which is less than the market price, in case if the stock fails to cross the strike price he will let his option unexercised and the premium can be retain by option seller.

When to use Covered Call strategy

When the investor holds the stock and he has neutral to moderately bullish view about the stock.

Risk & Reward associated with this strategy

The maximum risk an investor has with this strategy is stock price paid minus premium received on call sell. The stock can fall to lower levels but he will retain the premium as call buyer will not exercise his right if stock falls. The upper side is capped at the strike price plus the premium received. If the stock rises above the strike price he will start making loss on call sold which will be compensated by the rise in a stock. The profit is capped after price rises above the strike price.

Breakeven

Stock price paid – Premium Received

Strategy: Covered Call

	Bajaj Auto Stock	2500
Call option	Strike Price	2700
Mr. Salman receives	Premium	40
	Breakeven (Stock price – Put option premium)	2460

The Payoff Schedule

Bajaj Auto Ltd. Closes at (Rs.) on expiry	Payoff from the stock (Rs.)	Payoff from the Call option (Rs.)	Net payoff from strategy(Rs.)
2000	–500	40	–460
2100	–400	40	–360
2200	–300	40	–260
2300	–200	40	–160
2400	–100	40	–60
2460	–40	40	0
2500	0	40	40
2600	100	40	140
2700	200	40	240
2800	300	–60	240
2900	400	–160	240
3000	500	–260	240

Buy Stock

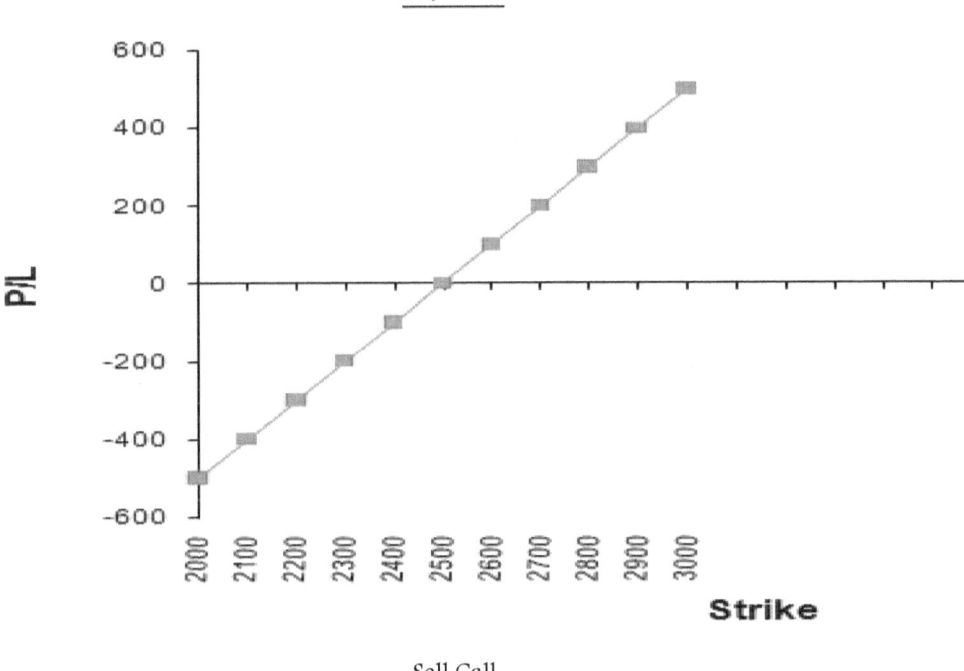

Sell Call

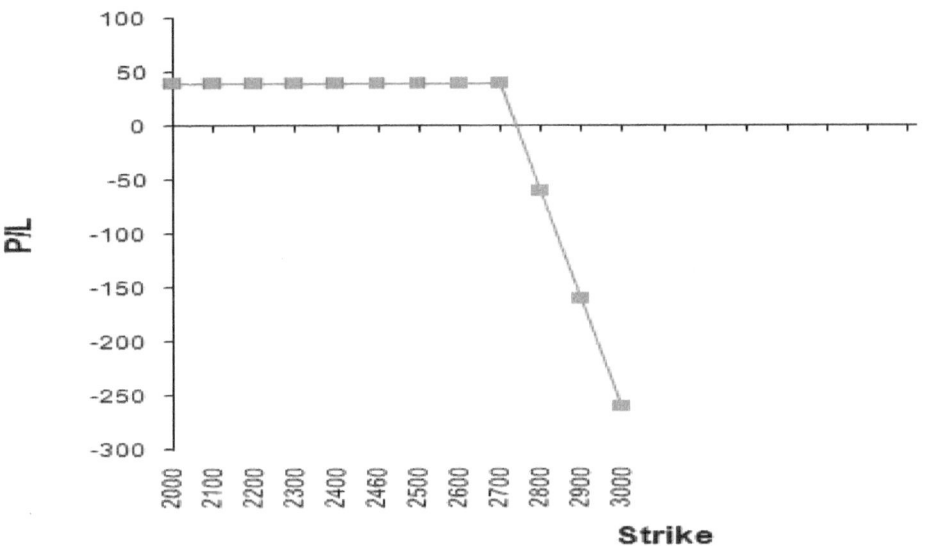

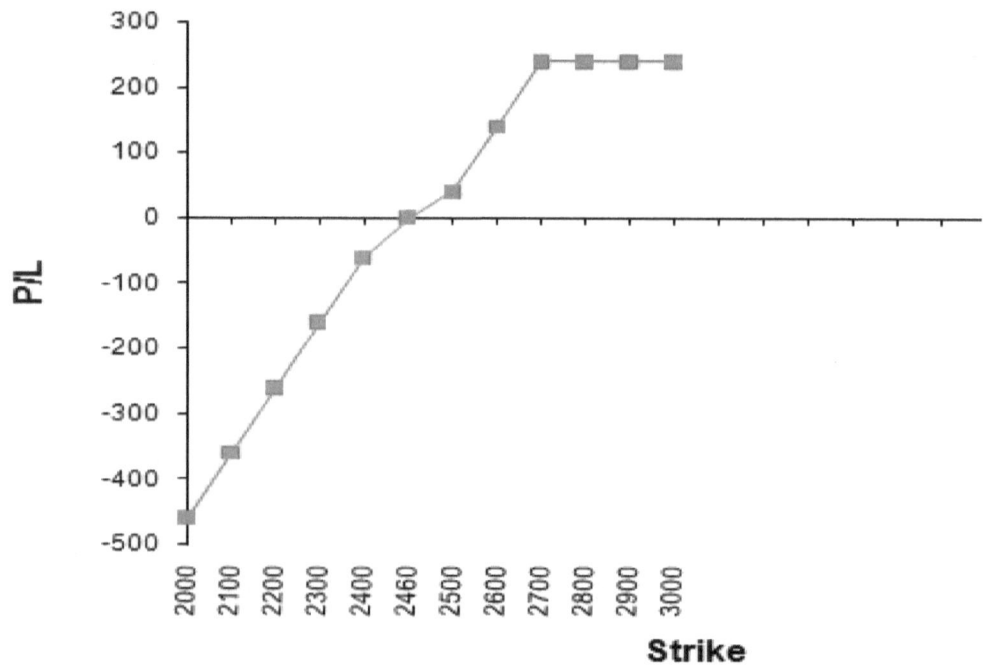

STRATEGY 7: LONG COMBO – SELL A PUT, BUY A CALL

The long combo is a bullish strategy and can be used instead of going long on the stock. The strategy produces the similar result as to rise in stock price. If an investor expects the stock price to rise in near future, he can do the long combo strategy instead of buying the stock and locking huge money on the stocks. The strategy is simply selling OTM (lower strike) Put and buying OTM (higher strike) call. As the stock price rises the strategy starts making profits.

Example- Mr. Aamir wants to buy the 1000 shares of Bharti Airtel at Rs.340 per share but instead of investing a huge amount on stocks he decided to use the long combo strategy. He sells a put option with a strike price of Rs.300 at a premium of Rs.1 and buys a call option with a strike price of Rs.380 at a premium of Rs. 2. The net cost of the strategy is Rs.1 (Rs.2 paid for buying the call- Rs.1 received on selling put).

Now if the stock rises above 381 which is a breakeven for the strategy (380 stock price+1 premium debit) Mr. Aamir will start making profit on the strategy. The profit can be unlimited to the extent the stock price rise. But if the stock prices starts to fall below 300 he starts to make losses which can be unlimited to the extent the stocks falls. The strategy is similar in payoff to long stock, except there is a gap between the strikes.

When to use Long Combo Strategy

When investor is bullish on stock and wants to take advantage of rise in stock price by investing a fraction of the stock amount.

Risk & Reward associated with this strategy

The risk & rewards are unlimited to the strategy. Payoffs are very similar to buying a stock.

Breakeven

Higher Strike + Net debit (380 + 1=381)

Strategy: Long Combo: Sell a Put buy a Call

	Bharti Airtel Stock price	340
Sells Put	Strike Price	300
Mr. Aamir receives	Premium	1
Buys call	Strike Price	380
Mr. Aamir Pays	Premium	2
	Net Debit (Premium paid – premium received)	1
	Breakeven (Higher Strike + Net Debit)	381

The Payoff Schedule

Bharti Airtel Ltd. Closes at (Rs.) on expiry	Net Payoff from the put sold(Rs.)	Net Payoff from the call purchased	Net payoff from strategy(Rs.)
240	–59	–2	–61
260	–39	–2	–41
280	–19	–2	–21
300	1	–2	–1
320	1	–2	–1
340	1	–2	–1
360	1	–2	–1
381	1	–1	0
400	1	18	19
420	1	38	39
440	1	58	59
460	1	78	79

Sell Put

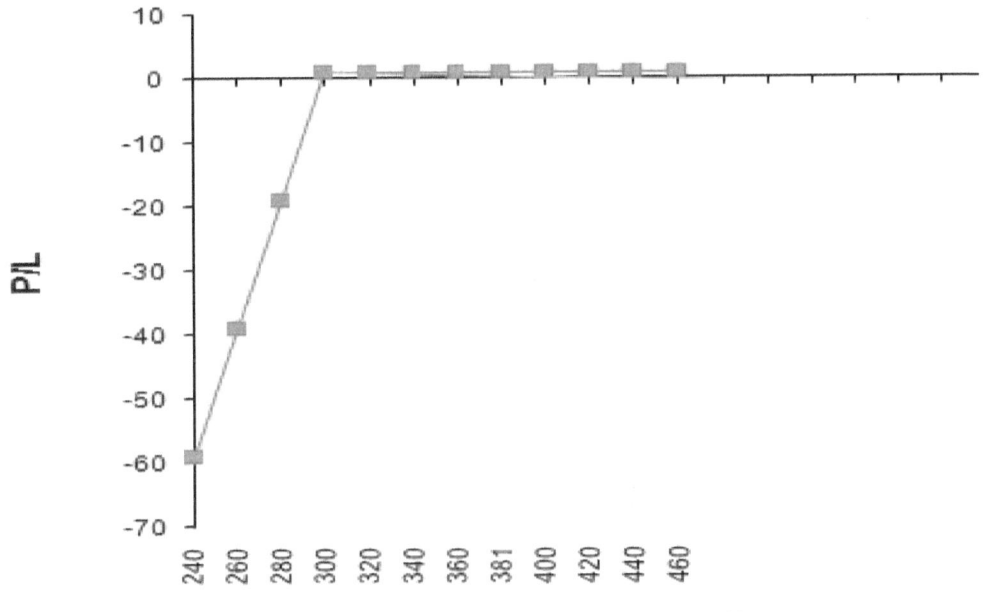

Buy Call

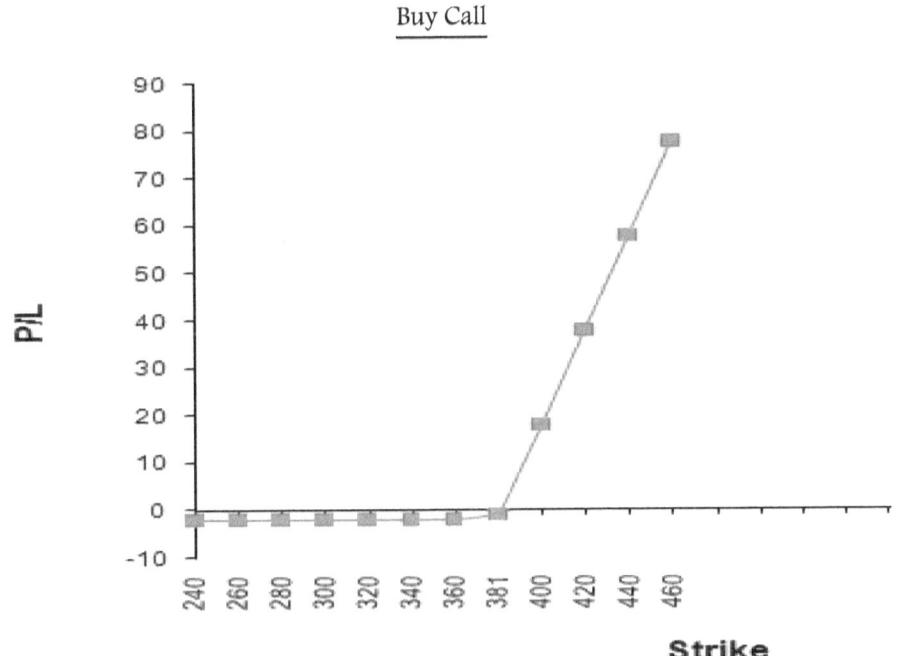

Long Combo Strategy

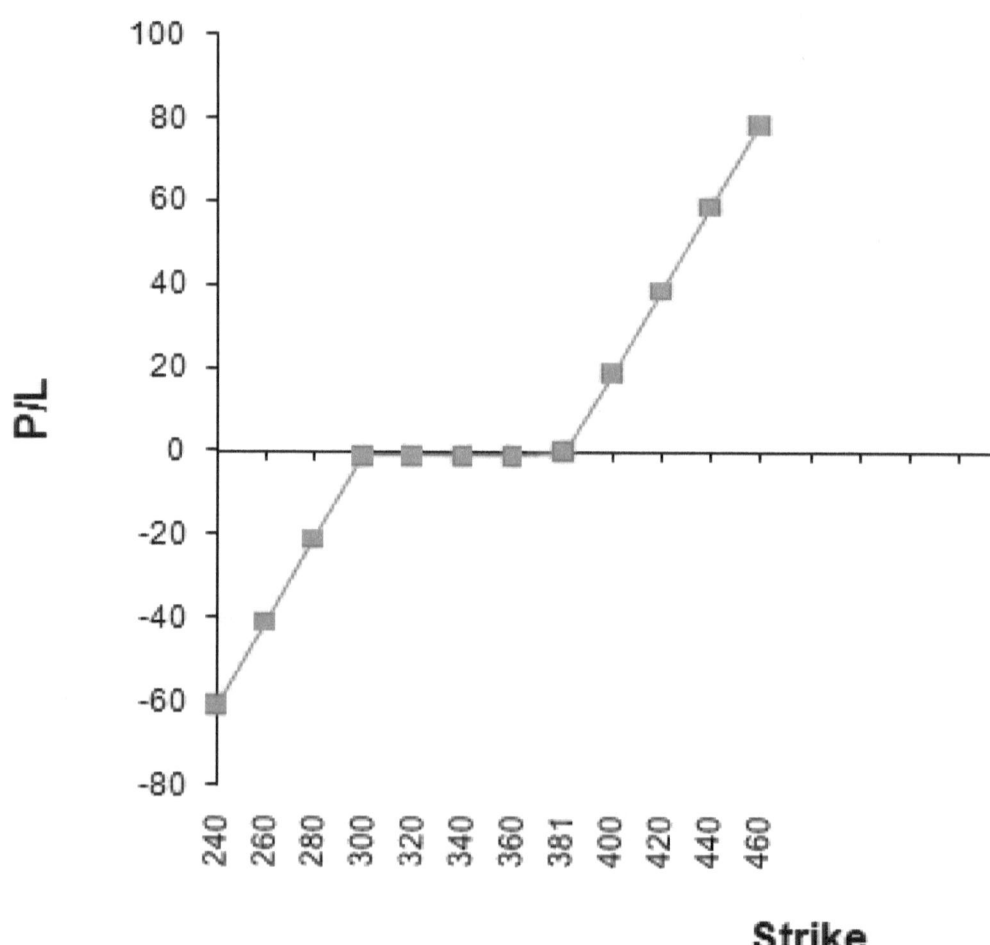

STRATEGY 8: PROTECTIVE CALL / SYNTHETIC LONG PUT

The protective call is an opposite of synthetic call strategy (strategy 3). When an investor is bearish on the stock but fears of any unexpected rise in the stock, protective call strategy is suitable for him. The strategy can be formulated by shorting a particular stock and buying ATM or slightly OTM call option. The payoff of the strategy is like long put but instead of having net debit (paying premium) for buying the put, he creates the net credit by shorting the stock and receiving money on the stocks. Now if the stock price falls he makes the profit but what if the stock price starts to rise? So he buys an ATM call to hedge his open position (short stock). By buying the call he limits his losses. If the stock price rises his pay off from the call option will increase and compensate him against the losses on shorting the stock. However the downside potential for profiting from the short stock will remain same. As the stock falls below breakeven level (stock price- call premium) the short position starts to makes profit.

Example- Mr. Abhishek shorts the nifty future at 6550 level but fears of rising prices in short term. To overcome his fear he decides to buy a call of strike price of 6600 at Rs.100 and hedge his short position. Now his break even will be Rs. 6450 (6550-100). He will start making profit when nifty falls below 6450. In this case his profit potential is maximum of the nifty falls below 6450 but his loss is limited to Rs.150 (6600-6550+100).

When to use Protective Call Strategy

When investor is bearish on the stock/index but wants to protect himself with any unexpected rise in prices.

Risk & Reward associated with this strategy

The risk is limited to the strategy.

Risk= Call Strike Price - Stock Price + Call Premium

Reward= Stock Price - Premium.

Breakeven

Breakeven = Stock Price – Call Premium

Strategy: Protective Call/Synthetic Long Put

(Short Stock + Buy Call Option)

Short Nifty	Current Market Price	6550
Buys Call	Strike Price	6600
Mr. Abhishek Pays	Premium	100
	Breakeven(Stock price- call premium)	6450

The Payoff Schedule

Nifty Future Closes at (Rs.) on expiry	Net Payoff from the stock (Rs.)	Net Payoff from the call purchased	Net payoff from strategy(Rs.)
5800	750	-100	650
5900	650	-100	550
6000	550	-100	450
6100	450	-100	350
6200	350	-100	250
6300	250	-100	150
6400	150	-100	50
6500	50	-100	-50
6550	0	-100	-100
6600	-50	-100	-150
6700	-150	0	-150
6800	-250	100	-150
6900	-350	200	-150
7000	-450	300	-150

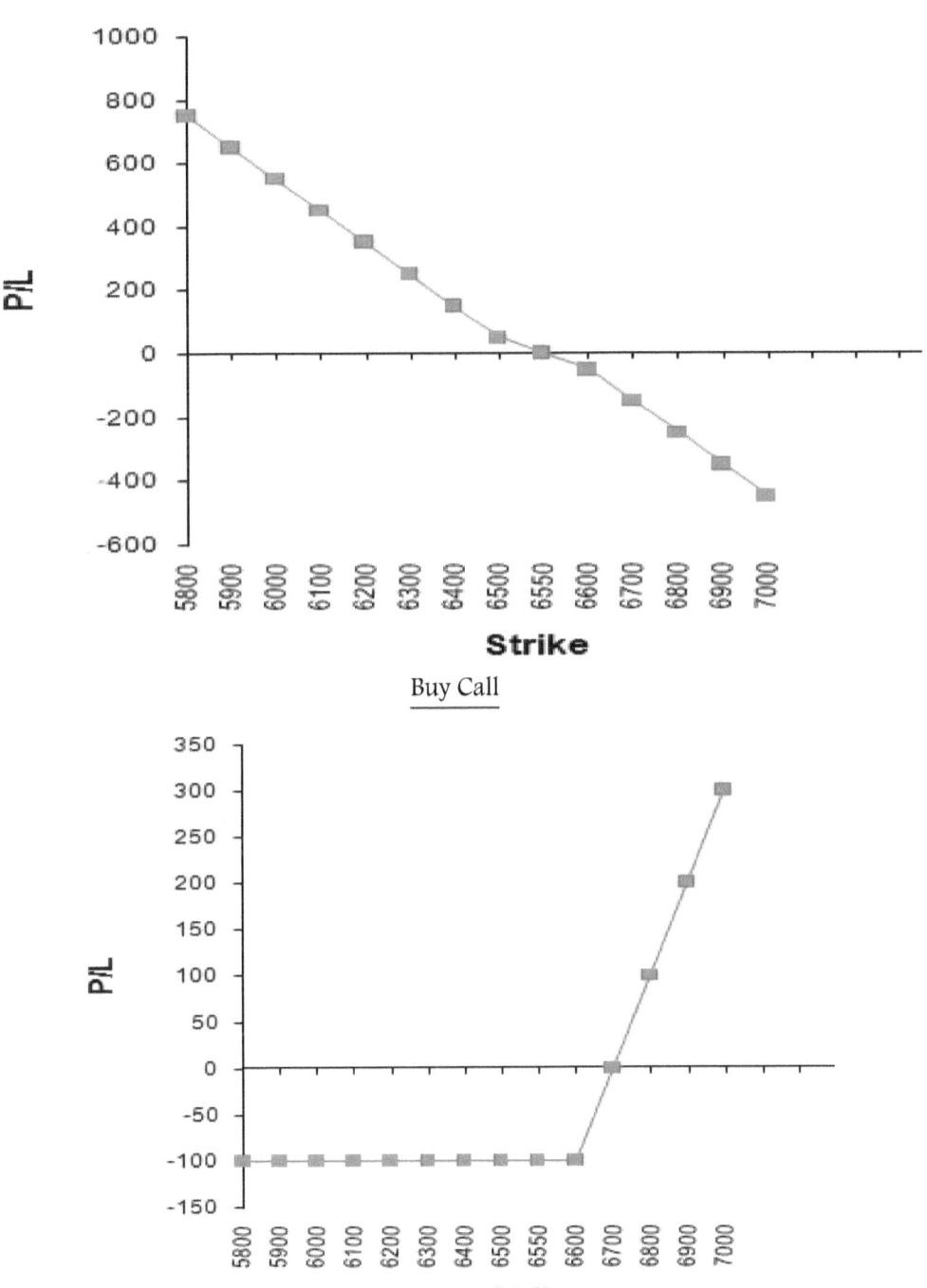

Protective Call/Synthetic Long Put

STRATEGY 9: COVERED PUT

The strategy is opposite to a covered call (Strategy 6). The strategy is suitable for the investors who are neutral to bearish on a particular stock/index. Investor sells the particular stock in anticipation that it will move down or remain sideways. Covered put strategy involves shorting a particular stock/index plus writing an OTM put option on the stock/index. Shorting the put means buying the stock at the strike price. When an investor shorts the stock he does not mind it buying it back at the strike price which is the target price for him. Selling put creates an obligation to buy the stock at the strike price if it were exercised by put buyer. The put buyer will only exercise the option if the stock/index falls below the strike price. In this case the put seller will be happy to buy the stock from put buyer at the strike price of the option because he has already sold the stock/index at higher prices. The strategy is named as covered put because he has already sold the stock and to cover his position he sells OTM put.

If the stock price does not change or remain above the strike price he will keep the premium of the put option, as the put option will expire at zero. The strategy provides an income to the investor in this scenario in the form of put premium.

Example- Ms. Kareena shorts the Bajaj Auto stock for Rs.2500 and shorts the put option of strike price of Rs.2300 at Rs.30. Ms. Kareena thinks that the stock may fall slightly near to Rs.2300 and her view is moderately neutral to bearish. She gets the premium of Rs.30 on the put sold and if the stock remains sideways between 2500-2300, she will retain the put premium as the put will expire at zero. By selling put Ms. Kareena creates a target for her short stock at Rs.2300. If the stock starts to fall below the strike price she will close his short position on the stock as she will be happy to buy the stock at the strike price gaining Rs.200 (2500-2300) on the stock.

When to use Protective Call Strategy

When investor is moderately bearish on a stock or index covered strategy is useful.

Risk & Reward associated with this strategy

The risk is unlimited to the strategy, if the stock price rises.

Maximum reward is (Stock sold Price – Strike Price) + Put Premium.

Breakeven

Breakeven= Stock sold price + Put Premium

Strategy: Covered Put

(Short Stock + Short Put Option)

Short Bajaj Auto	Current Market Price	2500
Sells Put	Strike Price	2300
Ms. Kareena Receives	Premium	30
	Breakeven(Stock sold price+ Put premium)	2530

The Payoff Schedule

Bajaj Auto Stock Closes at (Rs.) on expiry	Net Payoff from the stock (Rs.)	Net Payoff from the Put sold	Net payoff from strategy(Rs.)
2000	500	−270	230
2100	400	−170	230
2200	300	−70	230
2300	200	30	230
2400	100	30	130
2500	0	30	30
2530	−30	30	0
2600	−100	30	−70
2700	−200	30	−170
2800	−300	30	−270
2900	−400	30	−370
3000	−500	30	−470

Sell Bajaj Auto

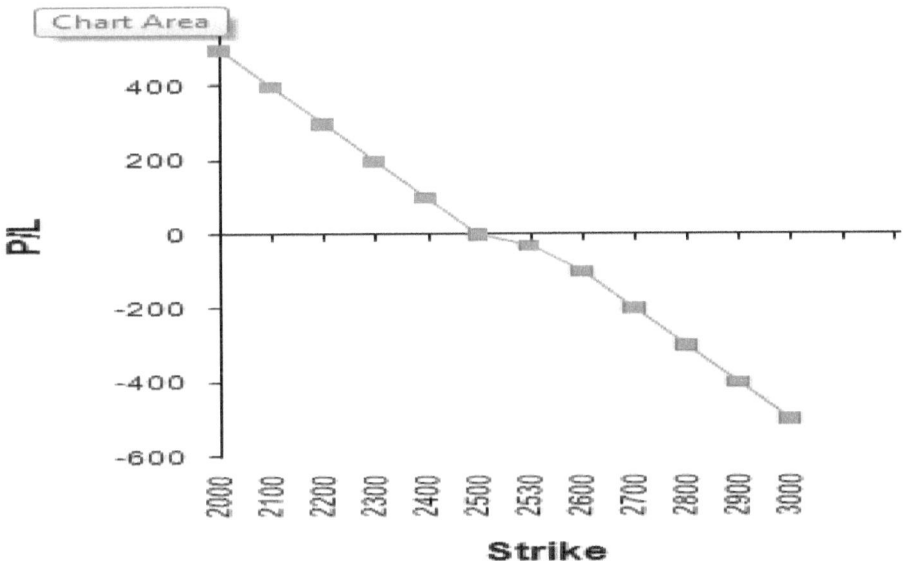

Sell Put

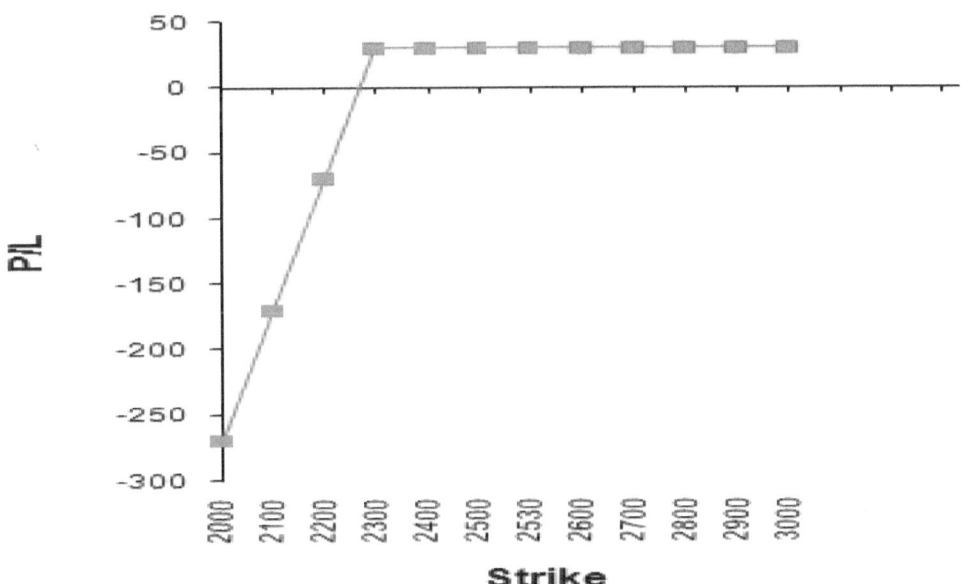

Covered Put

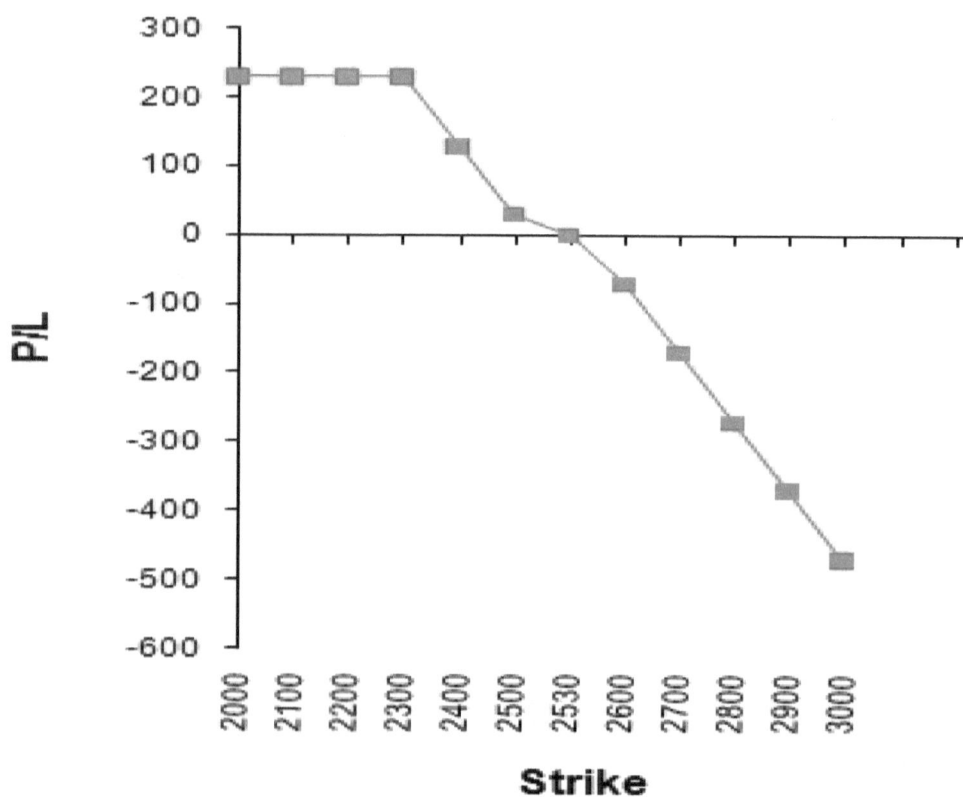

STRATEGY 10: LONG STRADDLE

The strategy is useful when an investor is neutral on the direction of the stock/index but expects a large movement in either direction. The strategy is formulated by buying a call as well as put on the same stock/index for the same maturity and same strike price. Investor hopes that the stock/index will be volatile and if it goes up he will earn from call and if it goes down the put will help him to earn money. He can exercise the call if stock/index hits high above the strike price of the options and similarly he can exercise the put option if market hits low below the strike price of the option. The only exception is stock/index must break out exponentially in either direction that the premium paid (cost of the trade) can be covered. If stock/index do not breakout in either direction or the breakout is not enough to cover the cost of the trade, the options will expire worthless.

Generally the options chosen are At the Money (ATM).

Example- Ms. Alia expects Nifty to be volatile in near term but doubts to which direction it will break. She buys nifty call option of strike price of Rs.7000 at Rs.110 and put option of strike price of Rs. 7000 at Rs. 70 when nifty is trading at 6950 level. Here the net debit to the strategy is Rs.180 (110+70), which is her maximum possible loss.

When to use Long Straddle

When investor expects the volatility in stock/index but doubts to which direction long straddle strategy is useful.

Risk & Reward associated with this strategy

The risk is limited to the premium paid for buying the options. The rewards can be unlimited as the nifty can rise or fall to any extent which leads increase in the price of either option (Call or put).

Breakeven

Upper Breakeven= Strike price of long call + Net premium paid
Lower breakeven= Strike price of long put − Net premium paid

Strategy: Long Straddle

(Long Call + Long Put)

Nifty Index	Current Market Price	6950
Buy Call & Buy Put	Strike Price	7000
Ms. Alia Pays Premium	Call+ Put (110+70)	180
	Upper Breakeven(7000+110)	7170
	Lower Breakeven(7000−70)	6930

The Payoff Schedule

Nifty Closes at (Rs.) on expiry	Net Payoff from the Call Purchased (Rs.)	Net Payoff from the Put Purchased (Rs.)	Net payoff from strategy(Rs.)
6500	−110	430	320
6600	−110	330	220
6700	−110	230	120
6820	−110	110	0
6900	−110	30	−80
7000	−110	−70	−180
7100	−10	−70	−80
7180	70	−70	0
7300	190	−70	120
7400	290	−70	220

7500	390	–70	320
7600	490	–70	420

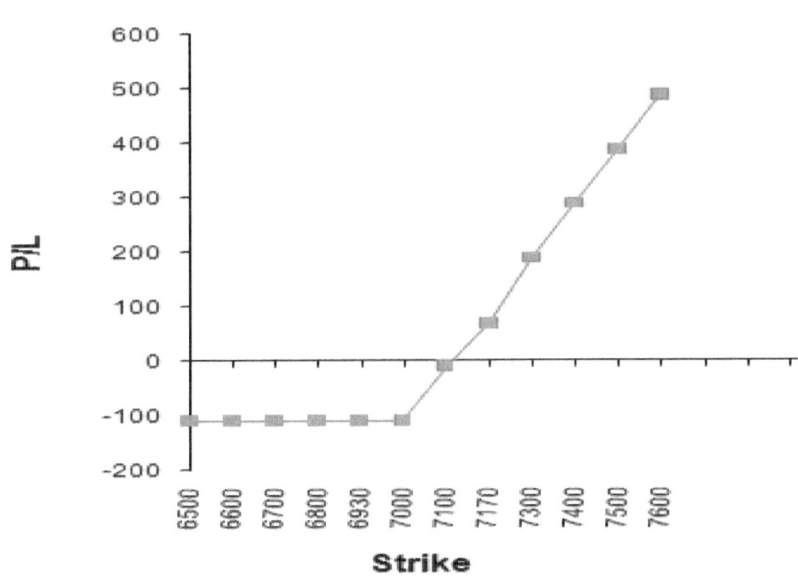

Nifty Call option

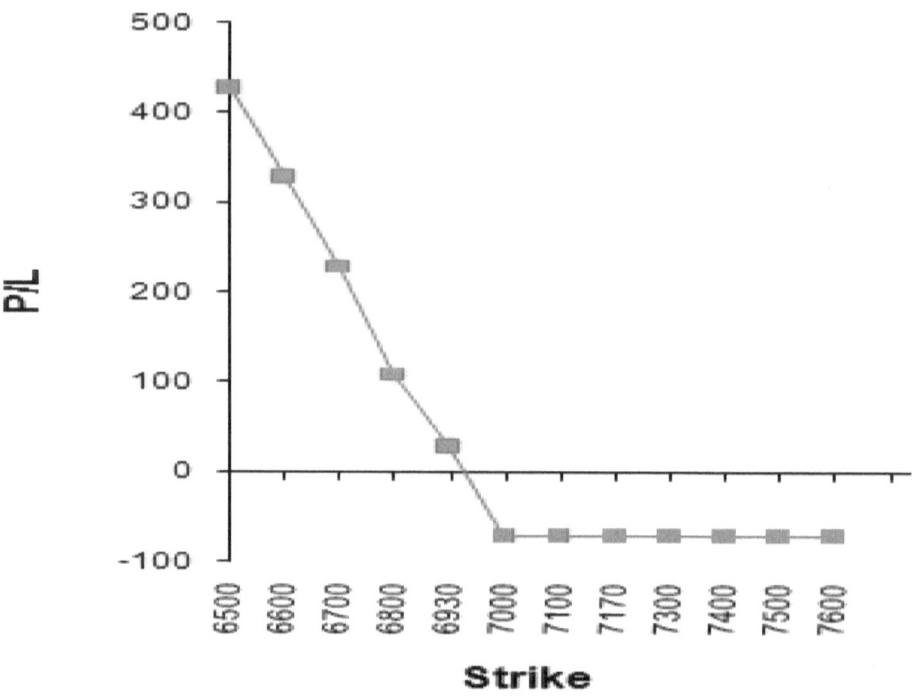

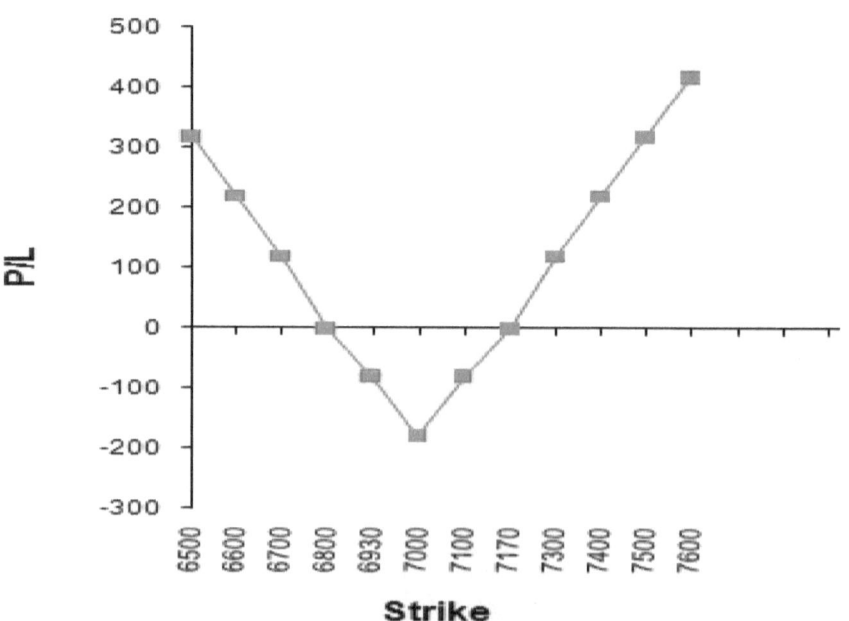

STRATEGY 11: SHORT STRADDLE

The short straddle strategy is useful when the investor feels that the volatility in the market is low and the market will not show much movement. The strategy is opposite of long straddle. The strategy is constructed by selling call and put of same stock/index for the same maturity and strike price. Generally the ATM (at the money) options are sold because they have maximum time value in it. The strategy creates the net income for the investor. Investor receives the premium on options sold and if the stock or index does not move much in either direction, the options will not be exercised by the option buyer and the option seller retains the premium as his income. The risk to the strategy is unlimited as the option can rise to any extent depending on the volatility. So the investor must keep in mind that this strategy should be adopted only when the volatility in the market is limited. The maximum gain is the premium received on selling options which can be possible if the stock/index closes at strike price of the contract.

Example- Mr. Ritesh expects nifty to be less volatile and in range bound. He decides to create short straddle by selling both call & put option of strike price of Rs.7000 at Rs.110 & Rs.70 when nifty is trading at 6950 level. Mr. Ritesh receives the net credit of Rs.180 which is his maximum possible profit from the strategy.

When to use Short Straddle

When investor expects the very less volatility in stock/index, he can adopt the short straddle strategy.

Risk & Reward associated with this strategy

The risk is unlimited as the stock/index can rise to any extent. The rewards are limited to the premium received.

Breakeven

Upper Breakeven= Strike price of short call + Net premium received
Lower breakeven= Strike price of short put – Net premium received

Strategy: Short Straddle

(Short Call + Short Put)

Nifty Index	Current Market Price	6950
Sell Call & Sell Put	Strike Price	7000
Mr. Ritesh Receives Premium	Call+ Put (110+70)	180
	Upper Breakeven(7000+110)	7170
	Lower Breakeven(7000-70)	6930

The Payoff Schedule

Nifty Closes at (Rs.) on expiry	Net Payoff from the Call Sold (Rs.)	Net Payoff from the Put Sold (Rs.)	Net payoff from strategy(Rs.)
6500	110	-430	-320
6600	110	-330	-220
6700	110	-230	-120
6820	110	-110	0
6900	110	-30	80
7000	110	70	180
7100	10	70	80
7180	-70	70	0
7300	-190	70	-120
7400	-290	70	-220
7500	-390	70	-320
7600	-490	70	-420

Nifty Call option

Nifty Put option

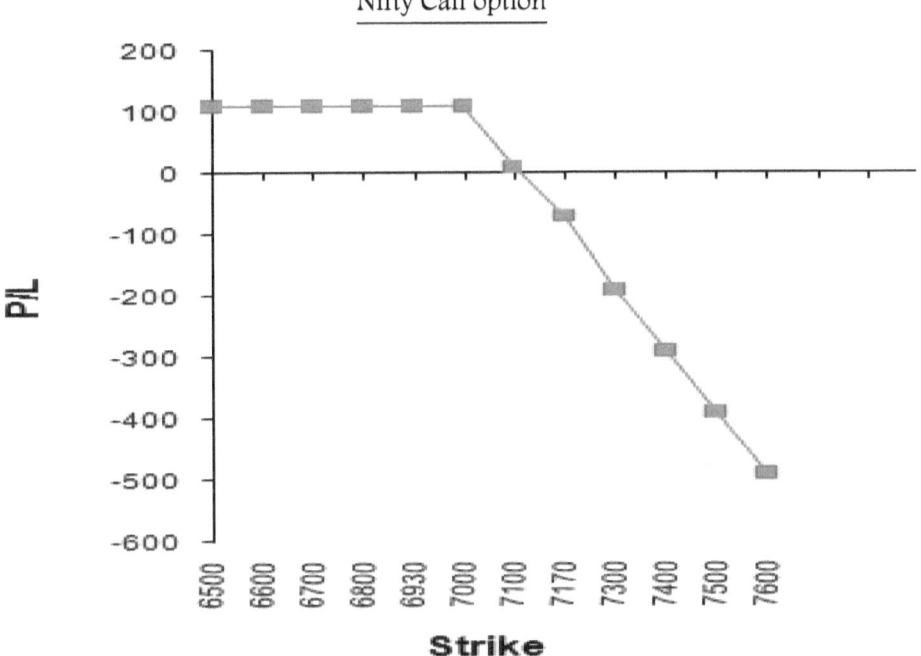

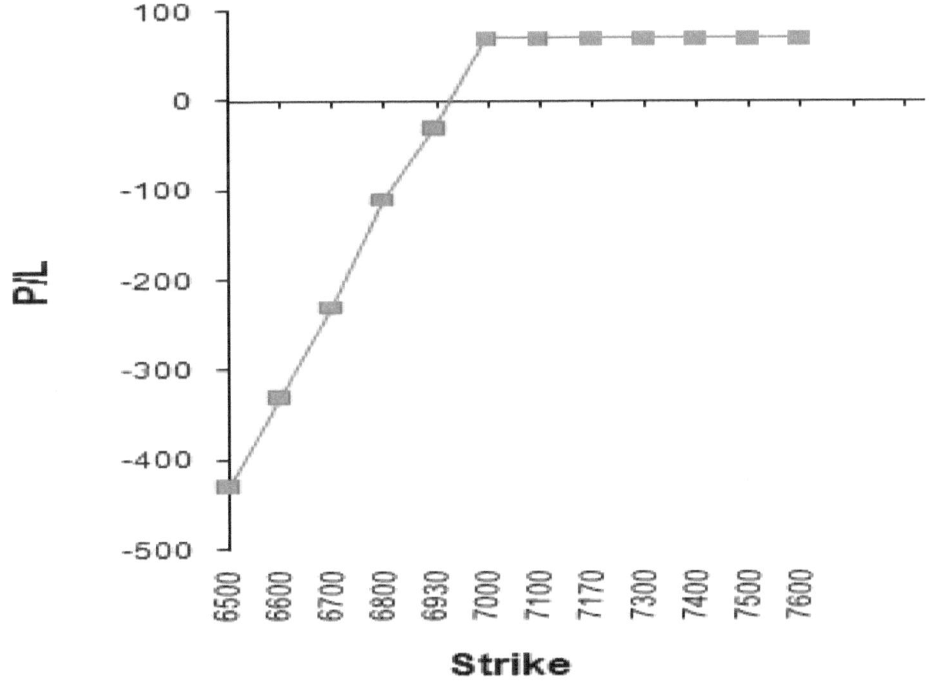

Short Straddle

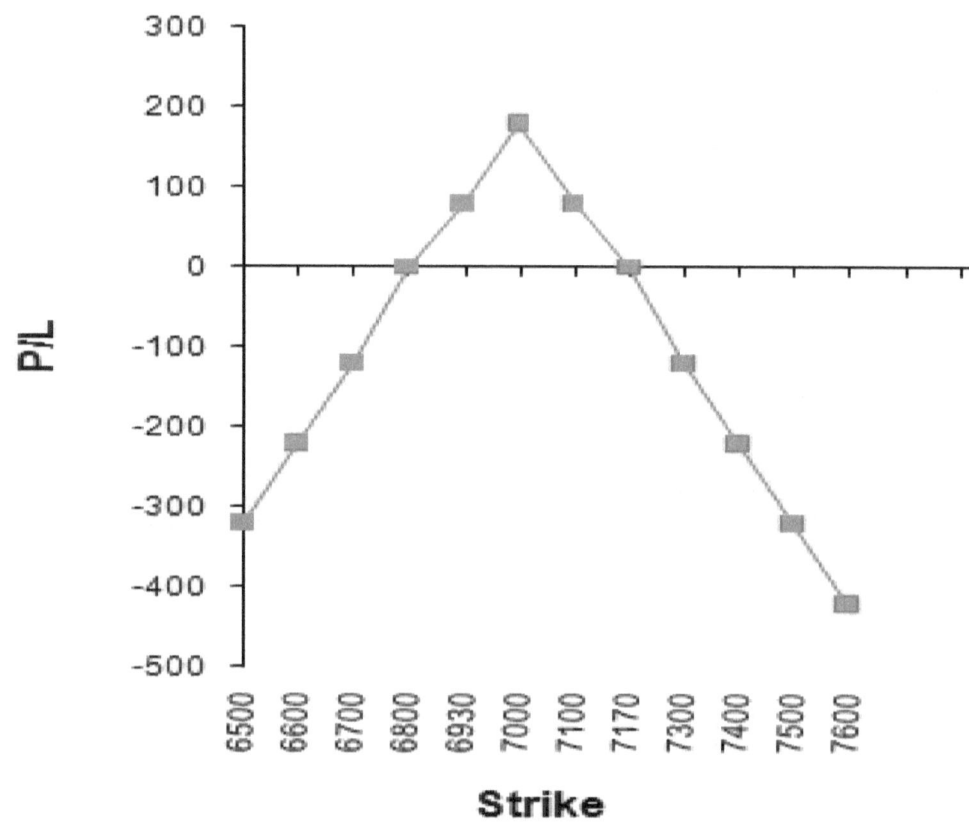

STRATEGY 12: LONG STRANGLE

Long strangle is an eversion to the long straddle which makes strategy cheaper than straddle. The strategy is constructed by buying a slightly out-of-the-money (OTM) put and an out-of-the-money call (OTM) of the same underlying stock/index and expiration date. Here the investor view is neutral on the direction of the stock/index but expects greater movement in either direction. The increased volatility would generate positive cash flow from either of the option. If the stock/index goes up significantly the call will be exercised by the investor, if it goes down than put will help him to generate returns from the strategy. As the OTM options (call & put) are purchased than ATM (at-the-money), this makes this strategy cheaper than straddle. However it requires a greater/increased movement in stock/index than it would be in straddle. The risk is limited to the premium paid for the strategy and returns are unlimited.

Example- Mr. Shahid expects a large movement in nifty but not sure in which direction. With limited resources in hand, he decides to enter in to a long strangle when nifty is trading at Rs.7000 by buying 7200 call at a premium of Rs. 50 and a put option of 6800 at a premium of Rs.40. The net debit to Mr. Shahid is Rs.90 (50+40) which is also his maximum possible loss.

When to use Long Strangle

When investor expects the volatility in stock/index but doubts to which direction long strangle strategy is useful. The strategy is cheaper than straddle as it involves OTM options.

Risk & Reward associated with this strategy

The risk is limited to the premium paid for buying the options. The rewards can be unlimited as the nifty can rise or fall to any extent which leads increase in the price of either option (Call or put).

Breakeven

Upper Breakeven= Strike price of long call + Net premium paid

Lower breakeven= Strike price of long put – Net premium paid

Strategy: Long Strangle

(Long OTM Call + Long OTM Put)

Nifty Index	Current Market Price	7000
Buy Call option	Strike Price	7200
Mr. Shahid Pays	Premium	50
	Upper Breakeven point (7200+50)	7250
Buy Put option	Strike Price	6800
Mr. Shahid Pays	Premium	40
	Lower Breakeven point	6760

The Payoff Schedule

Nifty Closes at (Rs.) on expiry	Net Payoff from the Call Purchased (Rs.)	Net Payoff from the Put Purchased (Rs.)	Net payoff from strategy(Rs.)
6500	–50	260	210
6600	–50	160	110
6700	–50	60	10
6760	–50	0	–50
6900	–50	–40	–90
7000	–50	–40	–90
7100	–50	–40	–90

7200	−50	−40	−90
7250	0	−40	−40
7400	150	−40	110
7500	250	−40	210
7600	350	−40	310

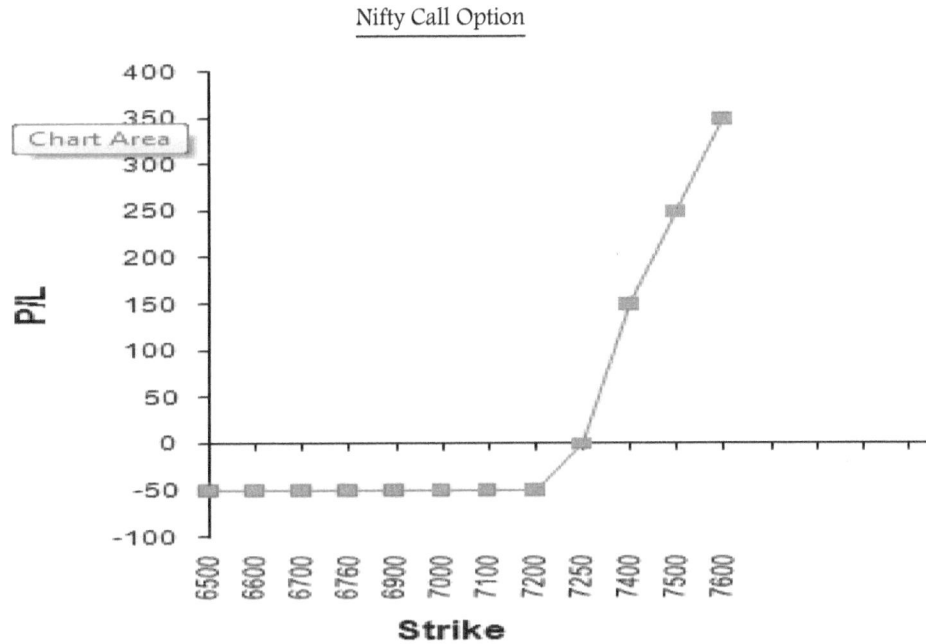

Nifty Put Option

Long Strangle

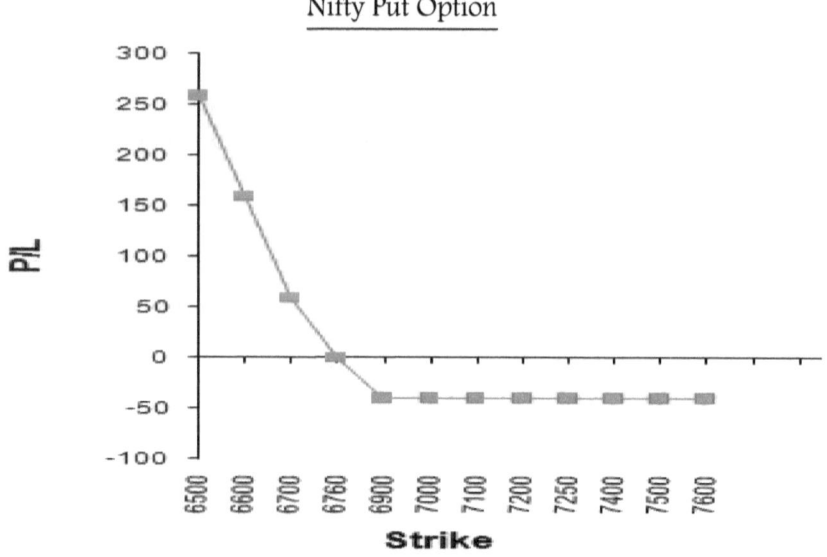

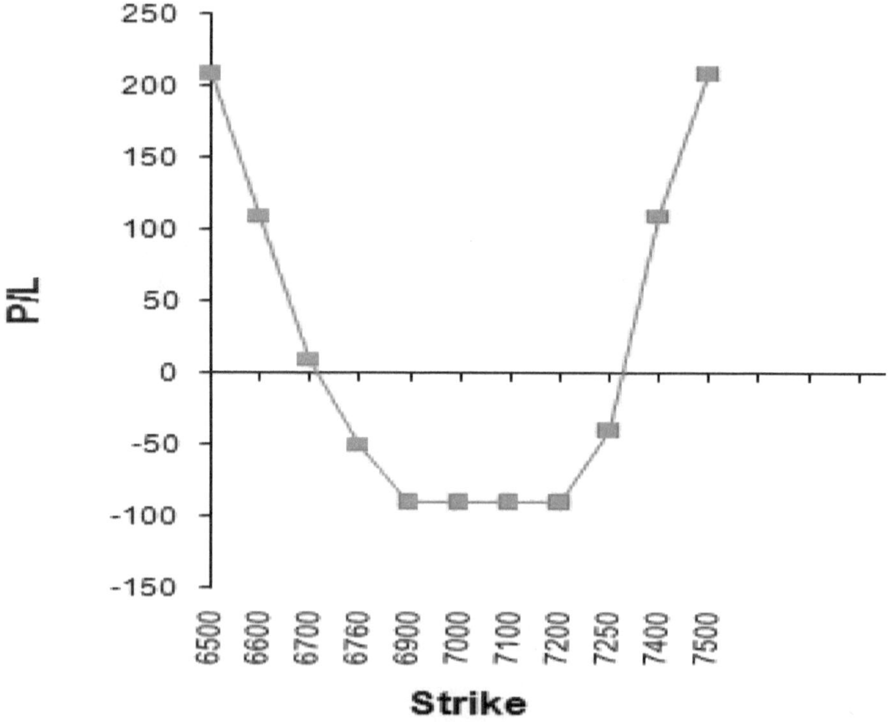

STRATEGY 13: SHORT STRANGLE

A short strangle is a modification of the short straddle strategy. The strategy is constructed by selling slightly out-of-the-money (OTM) call and slightly out-of-the-money put option of the same underlying and expiration date. The strategy reduces the risk of option seller by widening the breakeven points for option buyer. A much greater movement would be required in the underlying stock/index for the option to expire in-the-money. In short straddle the net credit receive by selling the options is higher than short strangle but the widening breakeven points for short strangle reduces the risk of options expiring in-the-money. If the underlying stock/index does not show much movement, the option seller will keep the premium as his profit for the option expiring worthless.

Example- When nifty is at 7500, Mr. Hrithik creates a short strangle by selling nifty 7300 put option for a premium of Rs. 30 and nifty 7700 call option for a premium of Rs. 45. The net credit by the strategy is Rs.75, which is also his maximum possible gain.

When to use Short Strangle

The strategy is useful when investor expects very low volatility in underlying stock/index. The strategy is cheaper than straddle as it involves OTM options.

Risk & Reward associated with this strategy

The risk is unlimited as the underlying can rise or fall to any extent thus options too can rise to any extent. The rewards are limited to the premium received.

Breakeven

Upper Breakeven= Strike price of short call + Net premium received

Lower breakeven= Strike price of short put − Net premium received

Strategy: Short Strangle

(Short OTM Call + Short OTM Put)

Nifty Index	Current Market Price	7500
Sell Call option	Strike Price	7700
Mr. Hrithik Pays	Premium	45
	Upper Breakeven point (7700+45)	7745
Sell Put option	Strike Price	7300
Mr. Hrithik Pays	Premium	30
	Lower Breakeven point (7300−30)	7270

The Payoff Schedule

Nifty Closes at (Rs.) on expiry	Net Payoff from the Call sold (Rs.)	Net Payoff from the Put sold (Rs.)	Net payoff from strategy(Rs.)
7000	45	−270	−225
7100	45	−170	−125
7200	45	−70	−25
7300	45	30	75
7400	45	30	75
7500	45	30	75
7600	45	30	75
7700	45	30	75
7800	−55	30	−85
7900	−155	30	−185
8000	−255	30	−285

Nifty Call Option

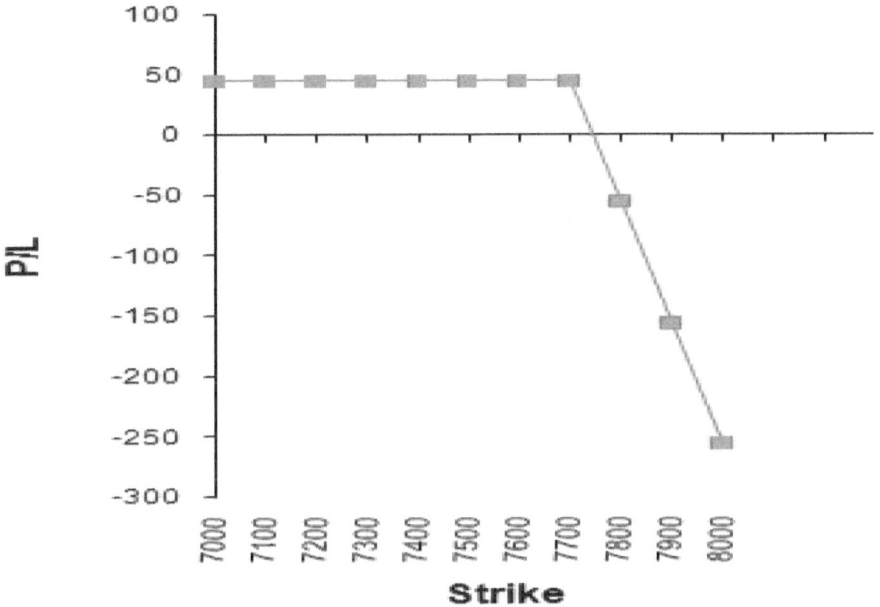

Nifty Put option

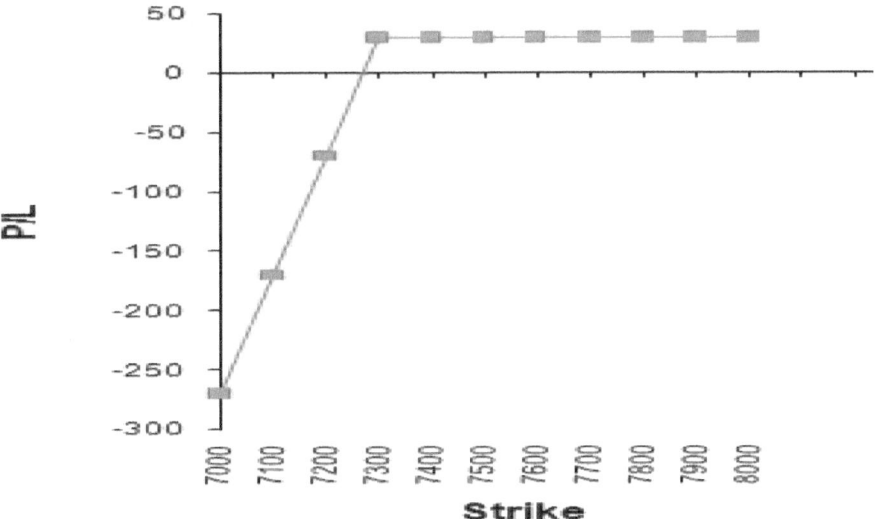

Short Strangle

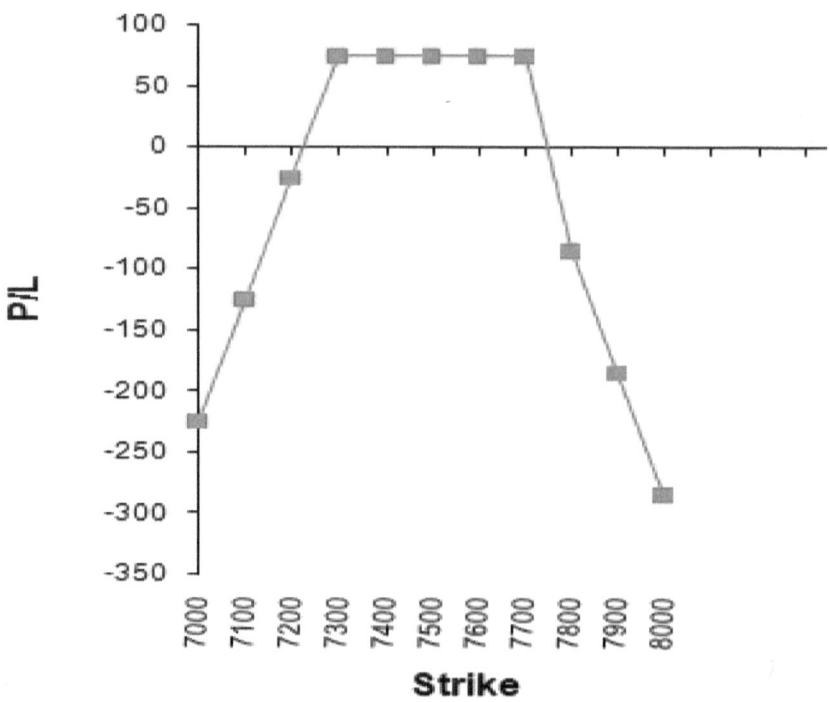

STRATEGY 14: COLLAR

A collar is buying a stock/index, then selling a call which creates covered call strategy and then insuring against the downside by buying a put. The strategy is very similar to covered call but involves another leg by buying a put. The put premium paid is partly financed by selling a call (premium received).

The strategy is conservatively bullish. The call (sold) prevents the opportunity of unlimited profit whereas on the other side the put prevents the downside risk. The put bought is generally ATM whereas the call sold is OTM, both having the same expiration month.

Example- Mr. Varun buys Maruti Suzuki stock at Rs.4000 and decides to establish a collar by writing a call of strike price of Rs.4200 for Rs. 10 and at the same time he buys a put with a strike price of Rs.3800 at Rs.5. Now he has paid Rs. 4000 per share for the stock, another Rs.5 for put purchased and receives Rs.10 as a premium on call sold. So his total investment per share is Rs. 3995. If lot size is 125 then he must buy at least 125 shares to establish a fair strategy.

When to use Short Strangle

The strategy is useful when investor is conservatively bullish and writing calls to earn premiums but wants to protect himself from a sharp fall in underlying price by buying a put.

Risk & Reward associated with this strategy

The risk and rewards are limited to the strategy. Call writing prevents the unlimited profit if underlying rises and put purchased limits the downside risk.

Breakeven

Purchase price of underlying – call premium received + Put premium paid

Strategy: Collar

(Buy Stock + Buy Put + Sell Call)

Maruti Suzuki	Current Market Price	4000
Sell Call option	Strike Price	4200
Mr. Varun Receives	Premium	10
Buy put Option	Strike Price	3800
Mr. Varun pays	Premium	5
	Net Premium Received (10-5)	5
	Breakeven point (4000-10+5)	3995

The Payoff Schedule

Maruti Suzuki Closes at (Rs.) on expiry	Net Payoff from the Call sold (Rs.)	Net Payoff from the Put Purchased (Rs.)	Net payoff from Stock (Rs.)	Net payoff from strategy(Rs.)
3500	10	295	-500	-195
3600	10	195	-400	-195
3700	10	95	-300	-195
3800	10	-5	-200	-195
3900	10	-5	-100	-95
4000	10	-5	0	5
4100	10	-5	100	105
4200	10	-5	200	205
4300	-90	-5	300	205
4400	-190	-5	400	205
4500	-290	-5	500	205

Call Option Sold

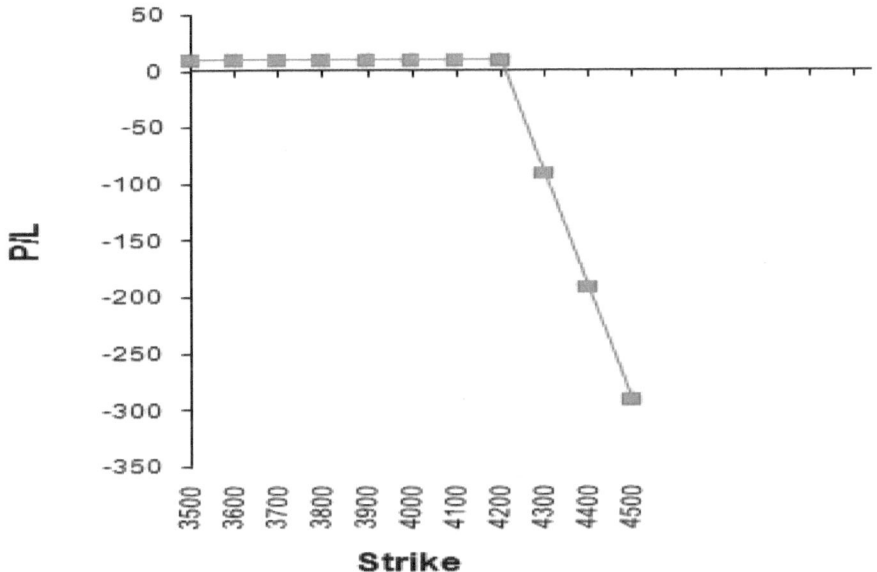

Put Option Purchased

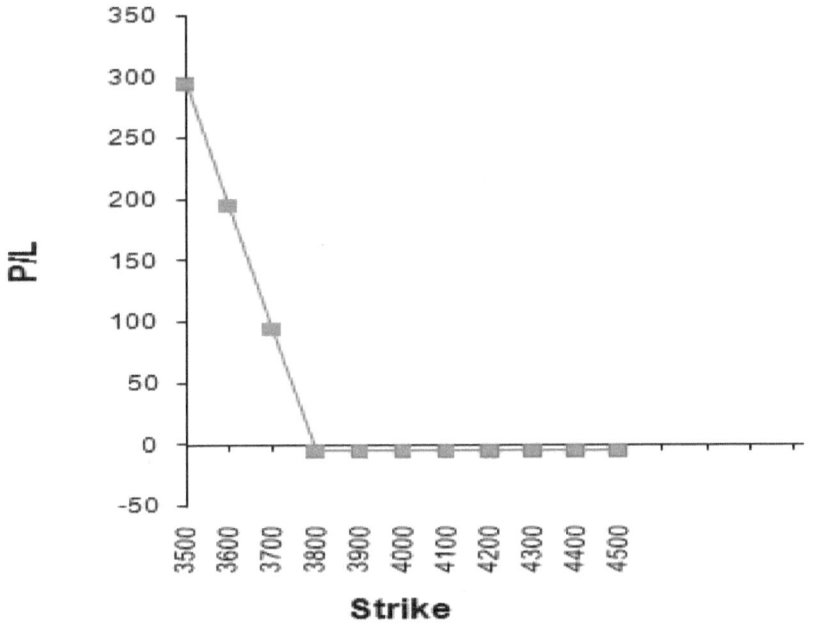

Buy Stock

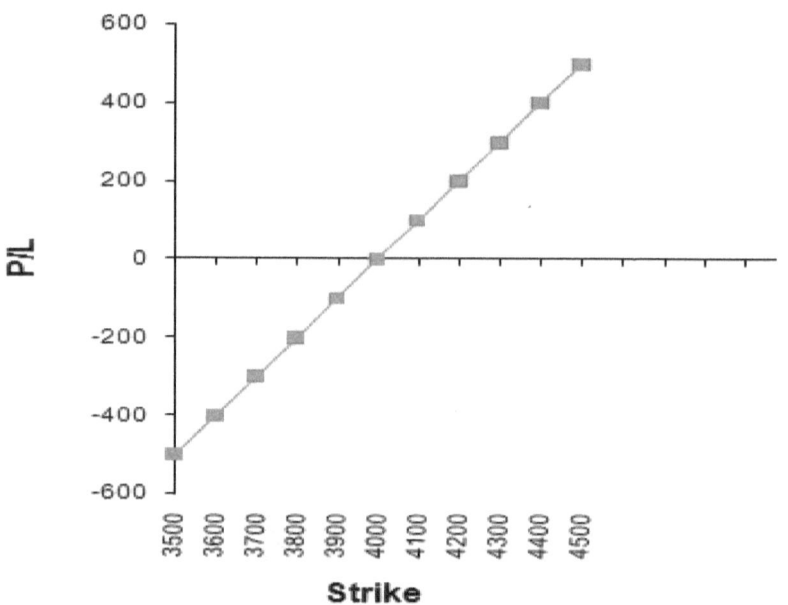

Collar Strategy

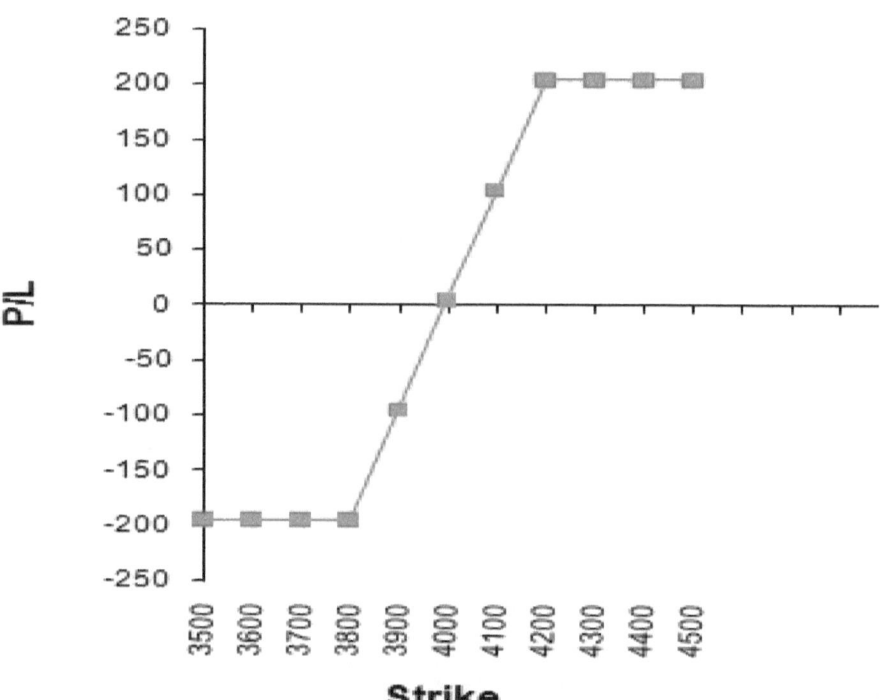

STRATEGY 15: BULL CALL SPREAD STRATEGY: BUY CALL OPTION, SELL CALL OPTION

A bull call spread strategy involves buying an in-the-money call (ITM) option and selling another out-of-the-money (OTM) call option, both with same expiration month and underlying. The strategy is moderately bullish and it reduces the cost of buying call option. Selling call reduces the cost of the strategy and investor remains the bullish or moderately bullish on the underlying.

The investor will make profit only when the underlying rises and makes loss if underlying falls. When underlying falls below ITM strike price, investor makes maximum loss and when underlying rises above OTM option he makes maximum profit.

Example- Mr. Farhan buys a call of strike price of Rs.7000 at a premium Rs.150 when nifty was at 7100. To reduce the cost or breakeven he sells the OTM call of strike price of 7400 at a premium Rs.50. The net debit to the strategy is Rs.100 (150-50=100) i.e. Rs.150 paid for buying call and Rs.50 received on call sold.

When to use bull Call Spread Strategy

The strategy is useful when investor is moderately bullish or bullish and wants to reduce the cost of the strategy.

Risk & Reward associated with this strategy

The risk & reward are limited to the strategy. Maximum loss occurs when underlying falls to the level of the lower strike price (ITM) or below. Similarly the maximum profit occurs where the underlying rises to the level of higher strike price (OTM) or above. The call sold limits the maximum profit as it starts to rise when underlying rises.

Breakeven

Strike price of purchased call + Net Debit paid.
(7000 + 100= 7100)

Strategy: Bull Call Spread

(Buy ITM Call + Sell OTM Call)

Nifty Index	Current Market Price	7100
Buy ITM Call Option	Strike Price	7000
Mr. Farhan Pays	Premium	150
Sell OTM Call Option	Strike Price	7400
Mr. Farhan Receives	Premium	50
	Net Premium Paid (150-50)	100
	Breakeven point (7000 +100)	7100

The Payoff Schedule

Nifty Closes at (Rs.) on expiry	Net Payoff from the Call Bought (Rs.)	Net Payoff from the Call Sold (Rs.)	Net payoff from Strategy(Rs.)
6500	-150	50	-100
6600	-150	50	-100
6700	-150	50	-100
6800	-150	50	-100
6900	-150	50	-100
7000	-150	50	-100
7100	-50	50	0
7200	50	50	100
7300	150	50	200
7400	250	50	300
7500	350	-50	300
7600	450	-150	300
7700	550	-250	300
7800	650	-350	300
7900	750	-450	300
8000	850	-550	300

Call Option Bought

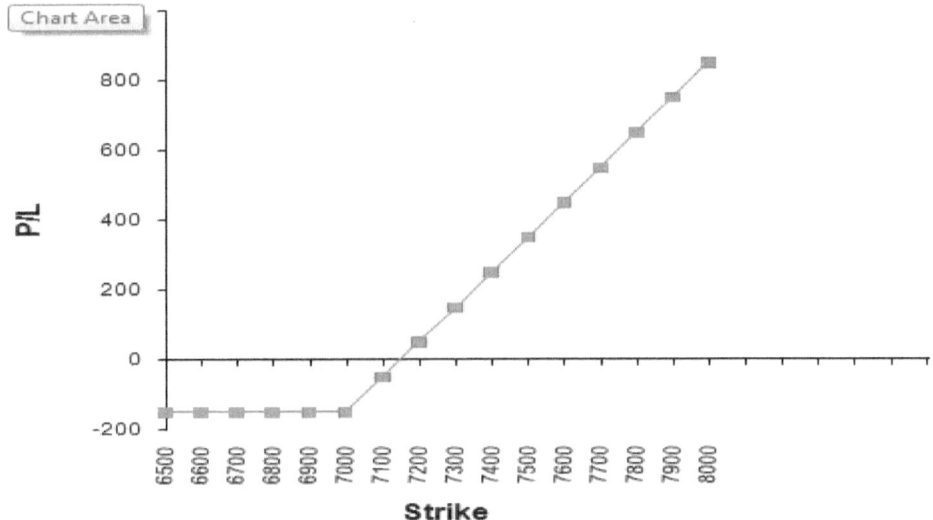

Call Option Sold

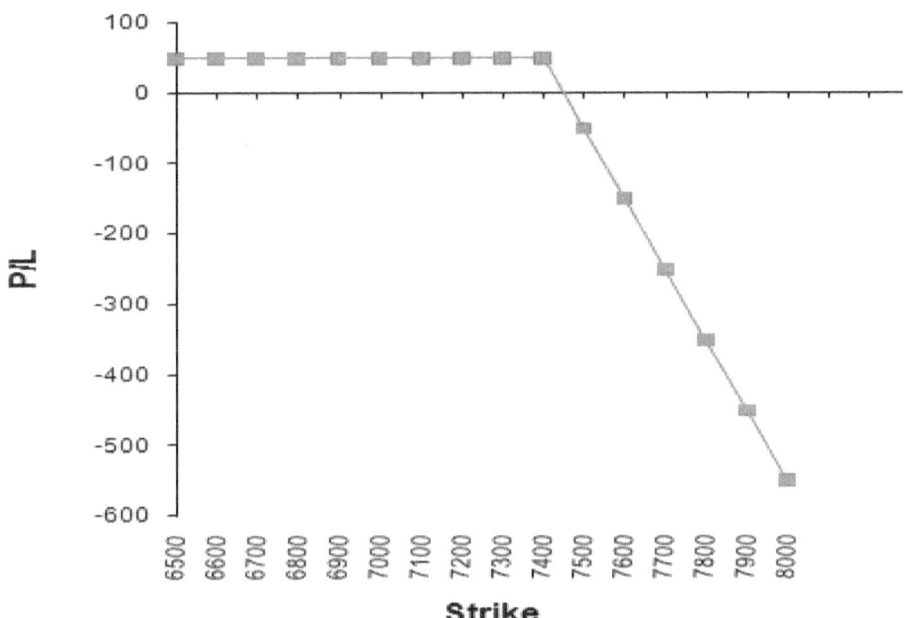

Bull Call Spread Strategy

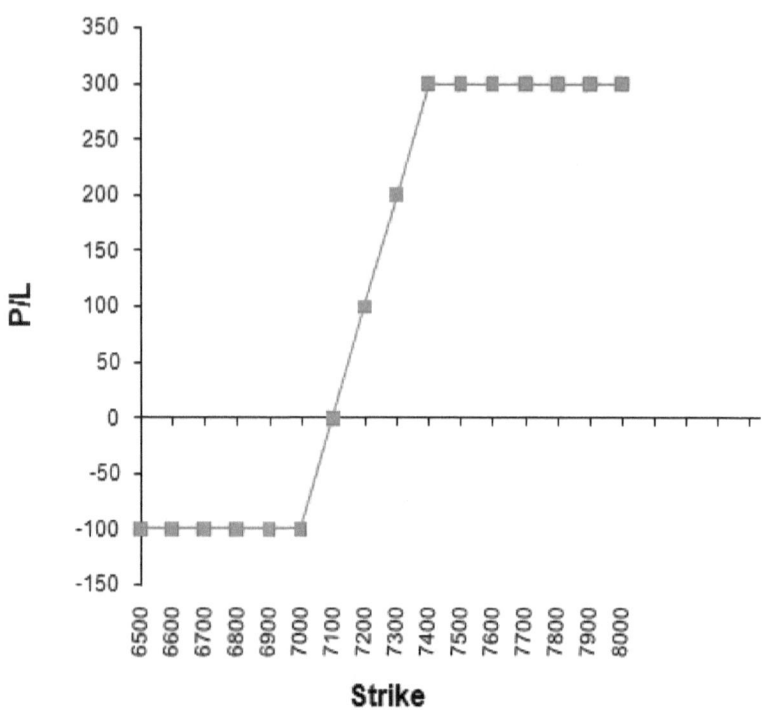

STRATEGY 16: BULL PUT SPREAD STRATEGY: SELL PUT OPTION, BUY PUT OPTION

A bull put spread strategy is useful for the investor who is moderately bullish on the underlying. When the underlying is expected to be range bound or rising, bull put spread strategy is profitable. The strategy is formulated by selling a higher strike price put option and then buying an OTM or lower strike price put option to protect the downside of a put sold. Here the investor receives the net credit as the put bought (OTM) is cheaper than the put sold (higher strike price). The strategy is similar to the bull call spread strategy but provides the income (net premium credited).

The strategy generates the income when the underlying rises, as both the puts expires worthless and the investor keeps the premium as a profit. If the underlying falls than the breakeven of the strategy will be higher strike price less net credit received. As long as underlying remains above breakeven level the investor profits. The maximum loss is the difference in strike less the net credit received.

Example- Ms. Katrina sells nifty 6000 strike option with a premium of Rs. 70 and buys an OTM put option with a strike price of 5800 at a premium of Rs. 30 to protect against the downside in underlying when nifty was trading at Rs.6200.

When to use bull Put Spread Strategy

The strategy is useful when investor is moderately bullish or underlying is range bound. The income is earned when the option sold expires worthless.

Risk & Reward associated with this strategy

The risk & reward are limited to the strategy. Maximum loss occurs where the underlying falls to the level of the lower strike or below. Maximum profit occurs where underlying rises to the level of the higher strike or above.

Breakeven

Strike price of short put − Net Premium received

(6000 − 40= 5960)

Strategy: Bull Put Spread

(Sell a Put + Buy a Put)

Nifty Index	Current Market Price	6200
Sell Put Option	Strike Price	6000
Ms. Katrina Receives	Premium	70
Buy Put Option	Strike Price	5800
Ms. Katrina pays	Premium	30
	Net Premium Received (70−30)	40
	Breakeven point (6000−40)	5960

The Payoff Schedule

Nifty Closes at (Rs.) on expiry	Net Payoff from the Put Buy (Rs.)	Net Payoff from the Put Sold (Rs.)	Net payoff from Strategy(Rs.)
5300	470	−630	−160
5400	370	−530	−160
5500	270	−430	−160
5600	170	−330	−160
5700	70	−230	−160
5800	−30	−130	−160
5900	−30	−30	−60
5960	−30	30	0
6000	−30	70	40
6100	−30	70	40
6200	−30	70	40
6300	−30	70	40
6400	−30	70	40
6500	−30	70	40

Put Option Bought

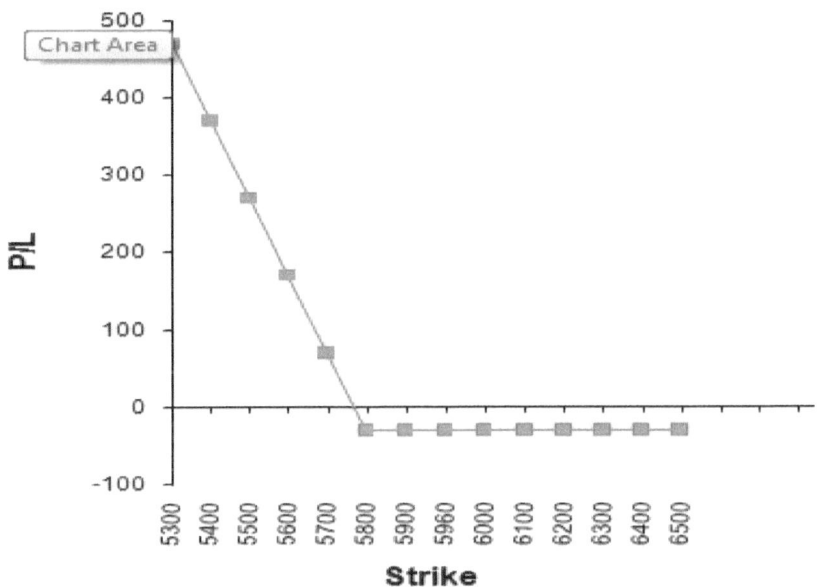

Put Option Sold

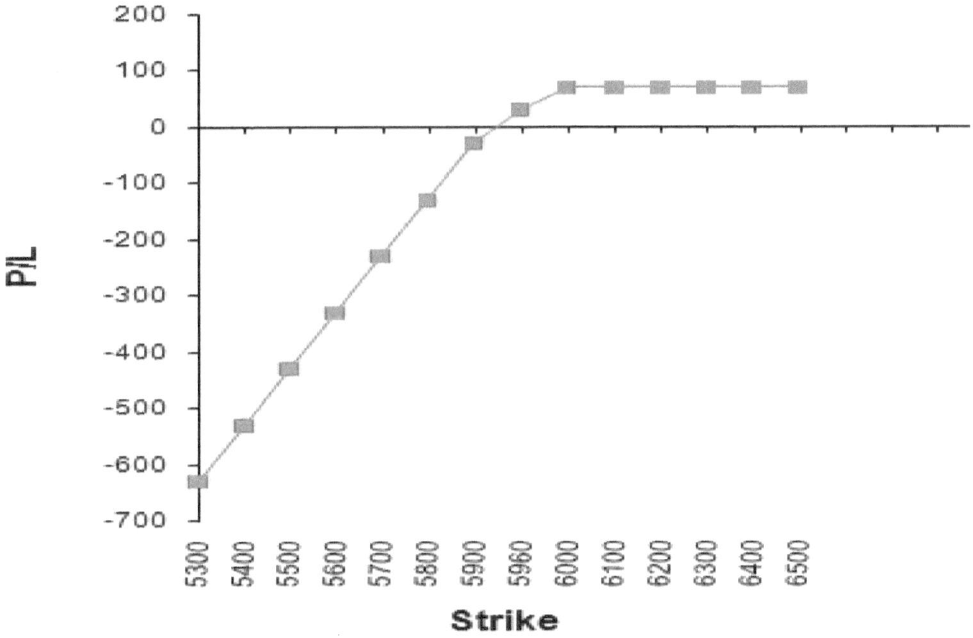

Bull Put Spread

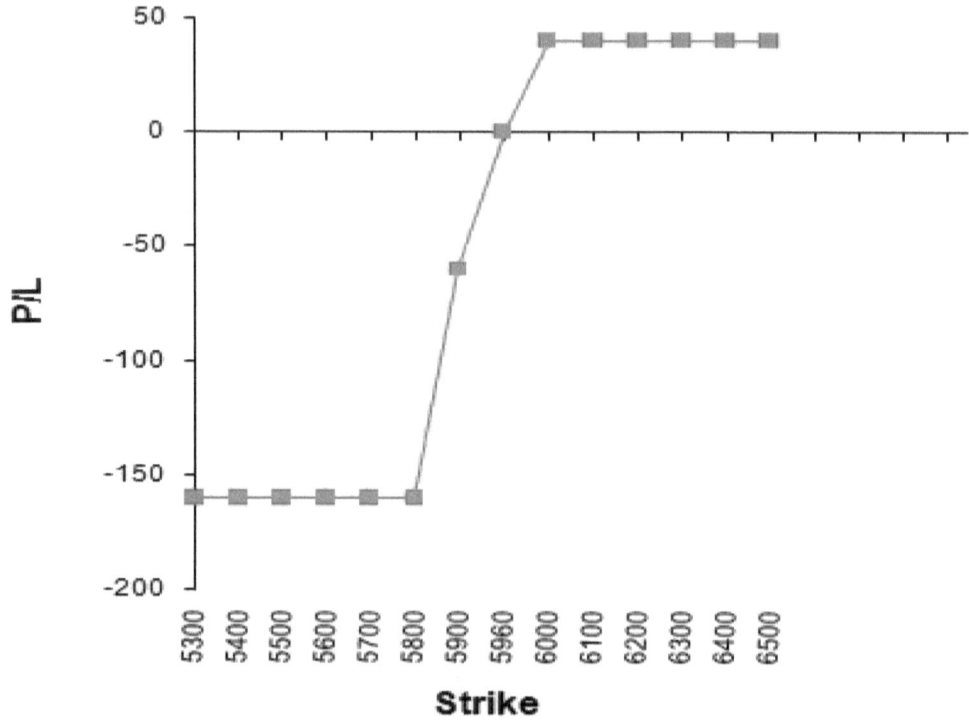

STRATEGY 17: BEAR CALL SPREAD STRATEGY: SELL ITM CALL & BUY OTM CALL

A bear call spread strategy involves selling ITM call option and buying OTM call option, both with same expiration month and underlying. The strategy is useful when investor is bearish on the underlying or expects range bound movement. The downside of call sold is insured by buying a call of higher strike price that is OTM call. The investor receives the net credit on this strategy because the call bought is of higher strike price than call sold. The strategy is also formulated with both OTM calls with the call bought is of higher OTM strike price than the call sold. The investor will retain the net credit if the underlying falls as both calls will expire worthless. If the underlying rises then the breakeven is the lower strike price plus the net credit. As long as the underlying remains below that level, the investor makes a profit. Otherwise he could make a loss. The maximum loss to the strategy is the difference in strikes less the net credit received.

Example- Ms. Alka is bearish on nifty and sells an ITM call option of strike price of 6900 at a premium of Rs.70 and buys an OTM call option of strike price of 7200 at a premium of Rs.25 when nifty was trading at 7000.

When to use Bear Call Spread Strategy

The strategy is useful when investor is mildly bearish on underlying or expects range bound movement.

Risk & Reward associated with this strategy

The risk & reward are limited to the strategy. Risk is limited to the difference between the two strikes minus the net credit. The reward is limited to the net credit received when options expires worthless.

Breakeven

Lower Strike + Net Credit

(6900 + 45 = 6945)

Strategy: Bear Call Spread

(Sell ITM/Lower Call option + Buy OTM/Higher Call option)

Nifty Index	Current Market Price	7000
Sell ITM Call Option	Strike Price	6900
Ms. Alka Receives	Premium	70
Buy OTM Call Option	Strike Price	7200
Ms. Alka pays	Premium	25
	Net Premium Received (70-25)	45
	Breakeven point (6900+45)	6945

The Payoff Schedule

Nifty Closes at (Rs.) on expiry	Net Payoff from the Call Sold (Rs.)	Net Payoff from the Call Bought (Rs.)	Net payoff from Strategy(Rs.)
6500	70	-25	45
6600	70	-25	45
6700	70	-25	45
6800	70	-25	45
6900	70	-25	45
6945	25	-25	0
7000	-30	-25	-55
7100	-130	-25	-155
7200	-230	-25	-255
7300	-330	75	-255
7400	-430	175	-255
7500	-530	275	-255
7600	-630	375	-255
7700	-730	475	-255

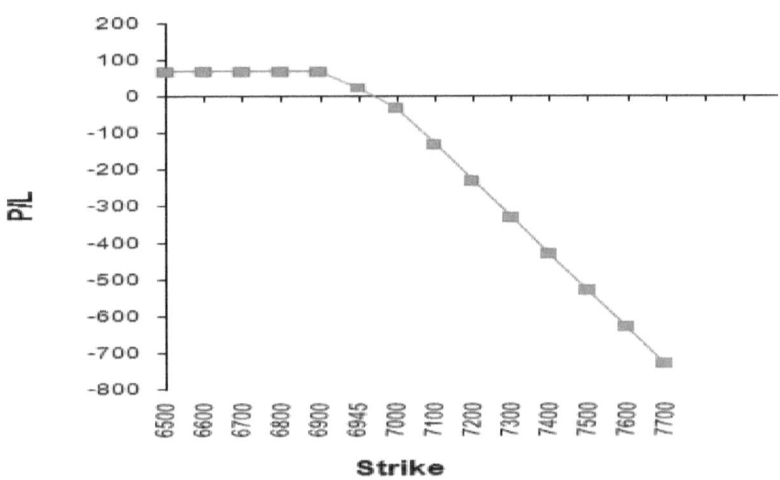

Sell ITM/Lower Strike Call

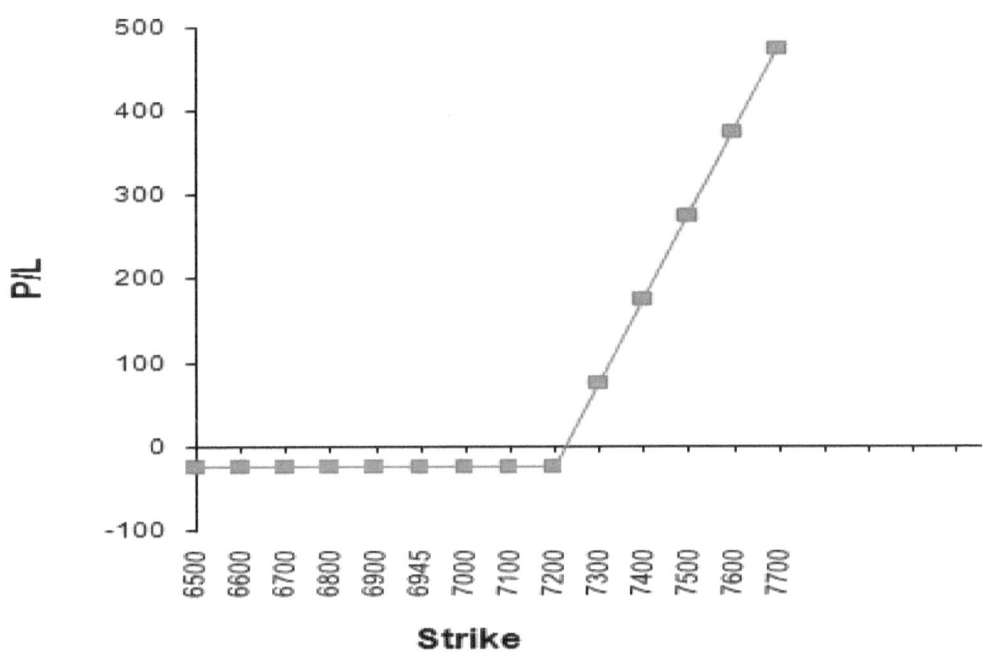

Buy OTM/Higher Strike Call

Bear Call Spread Strategy

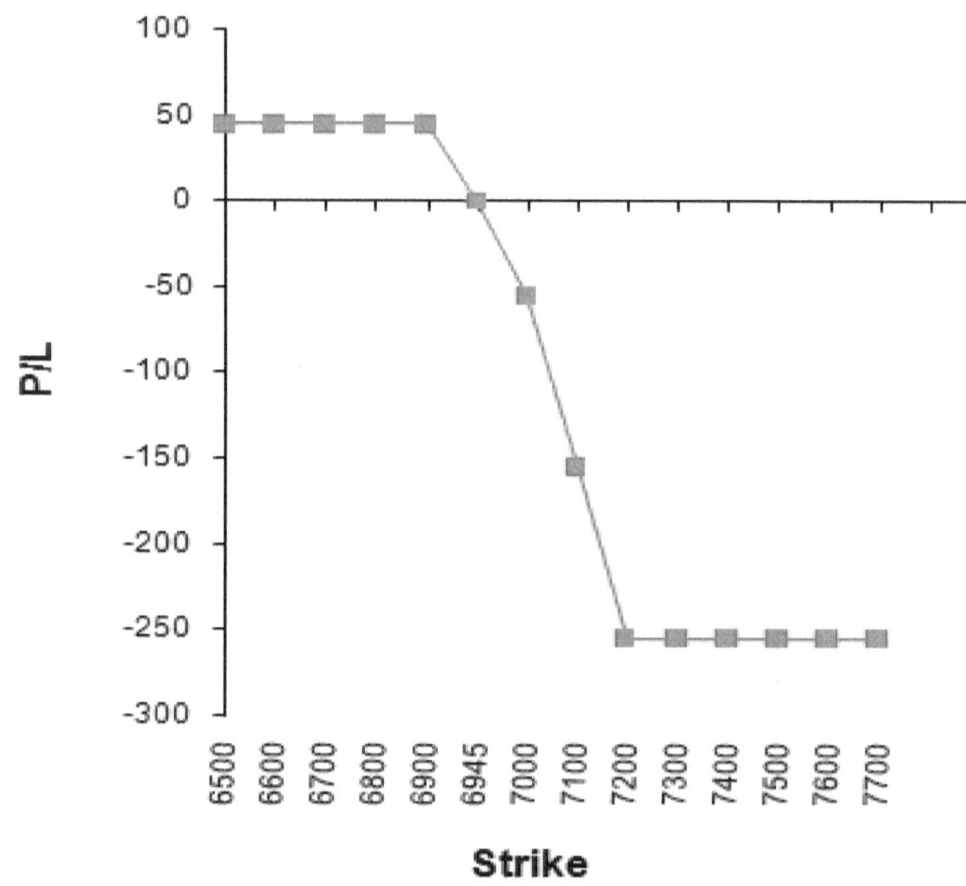

STRATEGY 18: BEAR PUT SPREAD STRATEGY: BUY PUT, SELL PUT

A bear put strategy is constructed by buying an ITM (higher strike) put option and selling OTM (lower strike) put option of the same underlying with same expiration period. The strategy is useful when investor is moderately bearish on underlying. The put bought will generate results when underlying will fall and the put sold will reduce the cost and raise the breakeven on buying a put. The strategy creates the net debit for the investor.

The maximum profit can be earned if underlying falls below the OTM (lower) put option strike price on expiration date. If the underlying increases above ITM (higher) put option strike price on expiration date, then the investor will have to bear a maximum loss which is equal to the net debit (premium paid) for the strategy.

Example- Mr. Imran is bearish on nifty and buys a nifty ITM put option with a strike price of 6300 at a premium of Rs. 170 when nifty was trading at 6180 and sells another OTM put option with a strike price of 6000 at a premium of Rs.50. the net debit to the strategy is Rs.120 (170-50).

When to use Bear Put Spread Strategy

The strategy is useful when investor is moderately bearish on underlying and expects underlying to fall.

Risk & Reward associated with this strategy

The risk & rewards are limited to the strategy. Risk is limited to the net debit paid for the strategy. Reward is limited to the difference between the two strike prices minus the net premium paid for the position.

Breakeven

Strike Price of Long Put – Net Premium Paid

(6300-120= 6180)

Strategy: Bear Put Spread

(Buy ITM/Higher strike Put option + Sell OTM/Lower strike Put option)

Nifty Index	Current Market Price	6180
Buy ITM Put Option	Strike Price	6300
Mr. Imran Pays	Premium	170
Sells OTM Put Option	Strike Price	6000
Mr. Imran receives	Premium	50
	Net Premium Paid (170-50)	120
	Breakeven point (6300-120)	6180

The Payoff Schedule

Nifty Closes at (Rs.) on expiry	Net Payoff from the Put Buy (Rs.)	Net Payoff from the Put Sold (Rs.)	Net payoff from Strategy(Rs.)
5600	530	-350	180
5700	430	-250	180
5800	330	-150	180
5900	230	-50	180
6000	130	50	180
6100	30	50	80
6180	-50	50	0
6300	-170	50	-120
6400	-170	50	-120
6500	-170	50	-120
6600	-170	50	-120
6700	-170	50	-120
6800	-170	50	-120

Buy ITM/Higher Strike Put

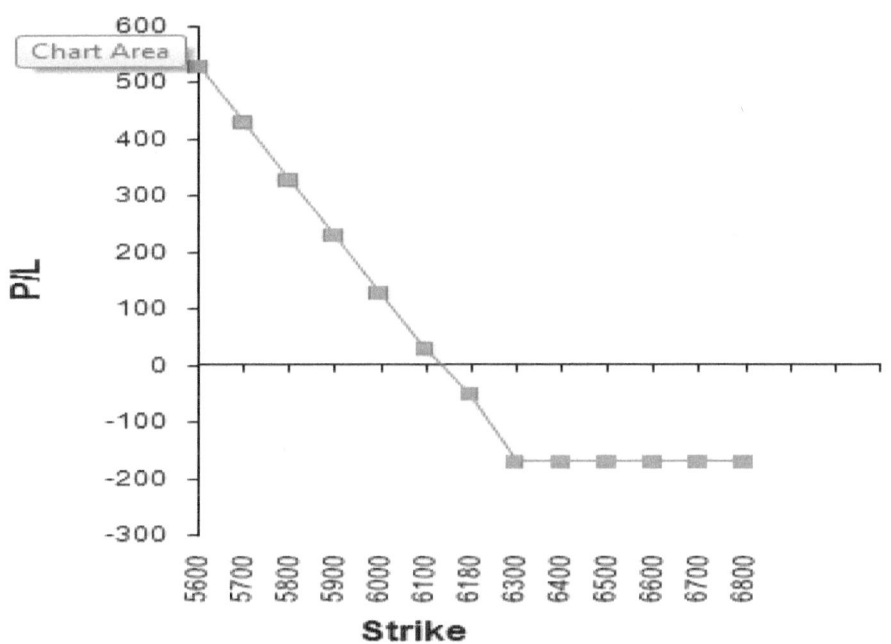

Sell OTM/Lower Strike Put

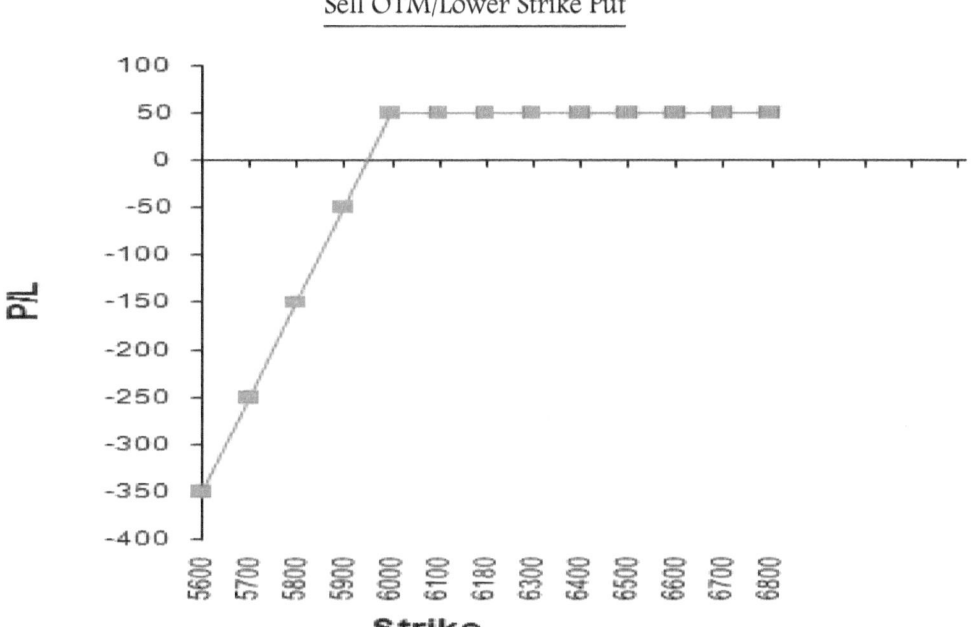

Bear Put Spread Strategy

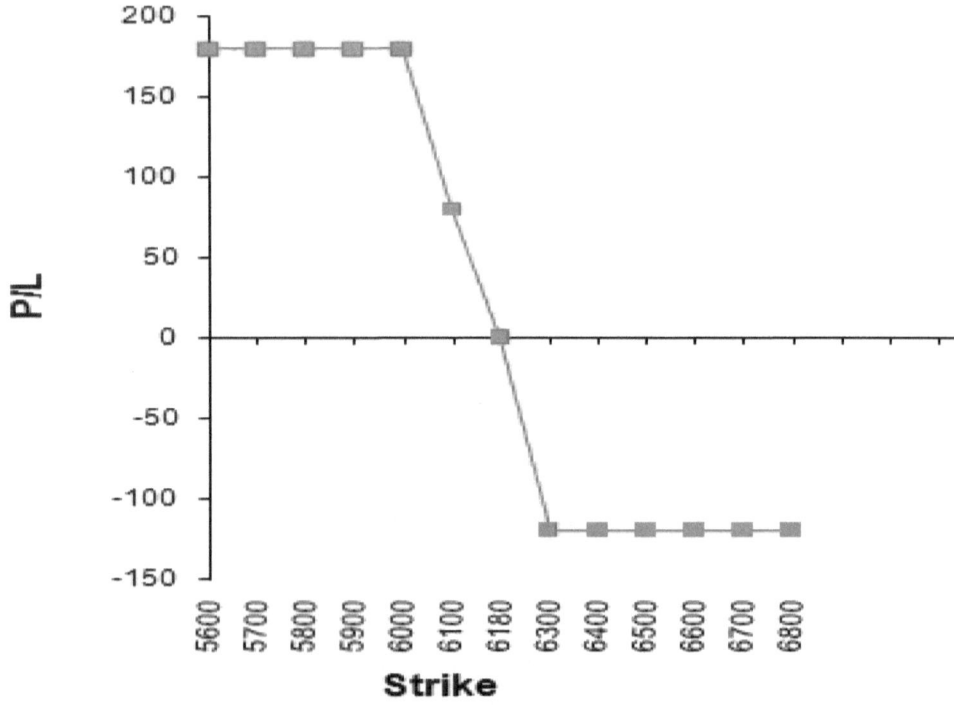

STRATEGY 19: LONG CALL BUTTERFLY: SELL 2 ATM CALL OPTIONS, BUY 1 ITM CALL OPTION AND BUY 1 OTM CALL OPTION

When the investor is expecting a very little movement in underlying, a long call butterfly strategy is useful to get benefit at a low cost. Due to the low volatility, the strategy offers a good risk/reward ratio together with low cost. The strategy is constructed by selling 2 ATM call options, buying 1 ITM call option and buying 1 OTM call option (with equal distance in strike prices). The strategy is very similar to short straddle except the losses are limited in case of long call butterfly.

The investor gains when the underlying remains range bound. The maximum profit can be earned if underlying remains at the middle strike price at expiration. The losses to the strategy are also limited.

Example- Mr. Shakti expects very little movement in nifty when nifty was trading at 7300. He decides to sell 2 ATM call options with a strike price of 7300 at a premium of Rs.100 each, buys 1 ITM call option with a strike price of 7200 at a premium of Rs. 150 and buys 1 OTM call option with a strike price of 7400 at a premium of Rs. 70. The net debit to the strategy is Rs.20.

When to use Long Call Butterfly Strategy

The strategy is useful when investor is neutral on the direction of the underlying and expects very low volatility.

Risk & Reward associated with this strategy

The risk & rewards are limited to the strategy. Risk is limited to the net debit paid for the strategy. Reward is limited to the difference between adjacent strike prices minus net debit.

Breakeven

Upper Breakeven Point = Strike Price of Higher Strike Long Call − Net Premium Paid

Lower Breakeven Point = Strike Price of Lower Strike Long Call + Net Premium Paid

Strategy: Long Call Butterfly

(Sell 2 ATM call option, Buy 1 ITM call option and Buy 1 OTM call option)

Nifty Index	Current Market Price	7300
Sell 2 ATM call option	Strike Price	7300
Mr. Shakti receives	Premium	100
Buy 1 ITM call option	Strike Price	7200
Mr. Shakti pays	Premium	150
Buy 1 OTM call option	Strike Price	7400
Mr. Shakti Pays	Premium	70
	Upper Breakeven Point (7400−20)	7380
	Lower Breakeven point (7200+20)	7220

The Payoff Schedule

Nifty Closes at (Rs.) on expiry	Net Payoff from 2 ATM Calls sold (Rs.)	Net Payoff from 1 ITM Call Purchased (Rs.)	Net Payoff from 1 OTM Call Purchased (Rs.)	Net payoff from Strategy(Rs.)
6700	200	−150	−70	−20
6800	200	−150	−70	−20
6900	200	−150	−70	−20
7000	200	−150	−70	−20
7100	200	−150	−70	−20
7200	200	−150	−70	−20
7220	200	−130	−70	0
7300	200	−50	−70	80

7380	40	30	-70	0
7400	0	50	-70	-20
7500	-200	150	30	-20
7600	-400	250	130	-20
7700	-600	350	230	-20

Sell 2 ATM Calls

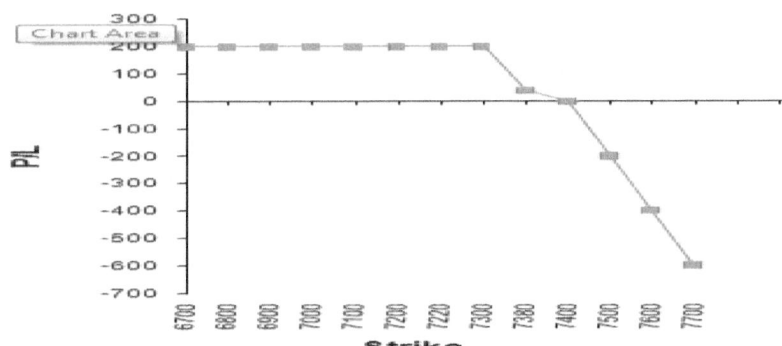

Buy 1 ITM Call

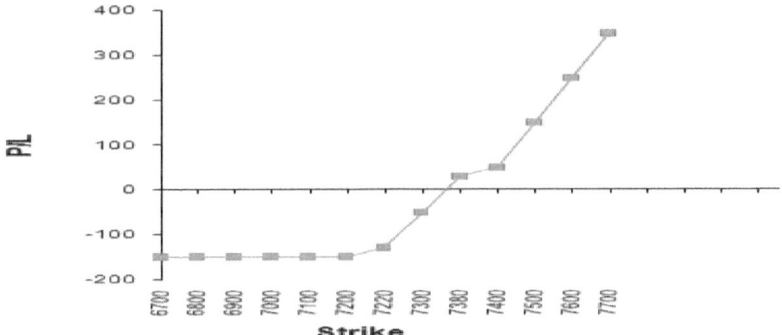

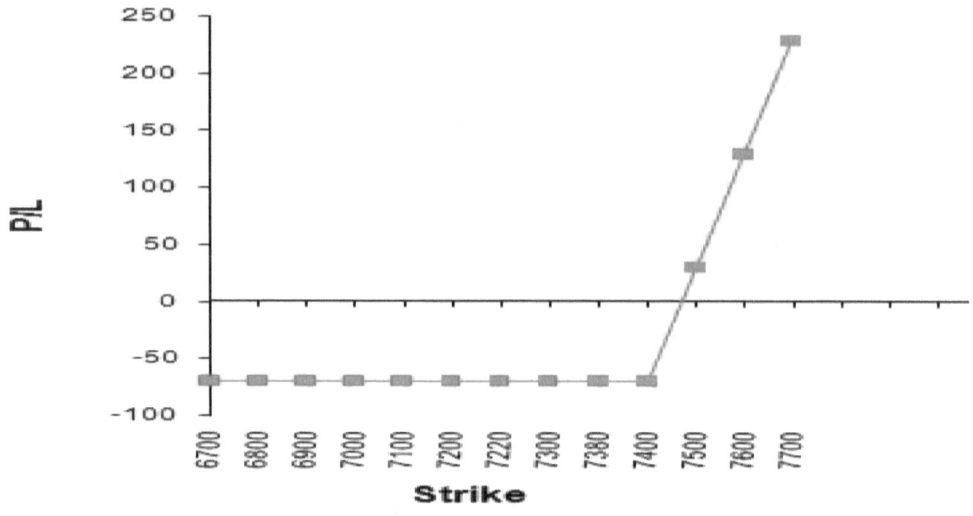

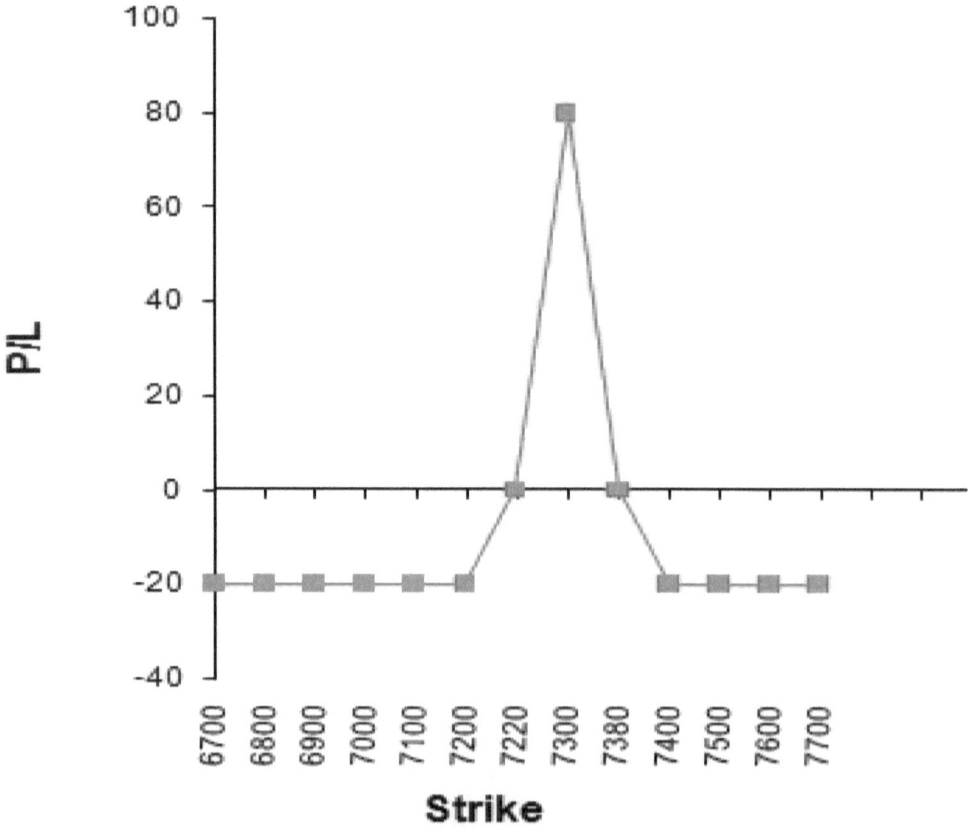

STRATEGY 20: SHORT CALL BUTTERFLY: BUY 2 ATM CALL OPTIONS, SELL 1 ITM CALL OPTION AND SELL 1 OTM CALL OPTION

When the investor is expecting a very large movement in underlying and the markets are volatile, short call butterfly strategy is useful to adopt. The strategy is just the opposite of long call butterfly. The short call butterfly strategy is constructed by buying 2 ATM call options, selling 1 ITM (lower strike) call option and selling another OTM (higher strike) call option. The strategy provides the net credit to the investor. The strategy produces profit in case there is a big move in the underlying. If the underlying expires at the middle strike the maximum risk occurs for the investor. The maximum profit can be earned if the underlying expires on either side of the upper and lower strike prices at expiration. The difference between each strike price must be equal. The strategy is slightly less risky than straddles and strangles and produces very small returns if compared to them.

Example- Mr.Vijay expects nifty to be very volatile in near term but doubts to which direction? He decides to enter in to a short call butterfly and buys 2 ATM call option of 7500 at a premium of Rs.100 each, sells 1 ITM call option of 7400 at a premium of Rs.150 and sells 1 OTM call option of 7600 at a premium of Rs. 70. Net credit to the strategy is Rs.20.

When to use Short Call Butterfly Strategy

The strategy is useful when investor is neutral on the direction of the underlying but expects high volatility.

Risk & Reward associated with this strategy

The risk & rewards are limited to the strategy. Risk is limited to the difference between the adjacent strikes less the premium received for the position. Rewards are limited to the net premium received from the options.

Breakeven

Upper Breakeven Point = Strike Price of Highest Strike short Call – Net Premium received

Lower Breakeven Point = Strike Price of Lowest Strike short Call + Net Premium received

Strategy: Short Call Butterfly

(Buy 2 ATM call options, Sell 1 ITM call option and sell 1 OTM call option)

Nifty Index	Current Market Price	7500
Buy 2 ATM call option	Strike Price	7500
Mr. Vijay Pays	Premium	100
Sell 1 ITM call option	Strike Price	7400
Mr. Vijay receives	Premium	150
Sell 1 OTM call option	Strike Price	7600
Mr. Vijay Receives	Premium	70
	Upper Breakeven Point (7600-20)	7580
	Lower Breakeven point (7400+20)	7420

The Payoff Schedule

Nifty Closes at (Rs.) on expiry	Net Payoff from 2 ATM Calls Bought (Rs.)	Net Payoff from 1 ITM Call Sold (Rs.)	Net Payoff from 1 OTM Call Sold (Rs.)	Net payoff from Strategy(Rs.)
7000	-200	150	70	20
7100	-200	150	70	20
7200	-200	150	70	20
7300	-200	150	70	20
7400	-200	150	70	20
7420	-200	130	70	0
7500	-200	50	70	-80
7580	-40	-30	70	0
7600	0	-50	70	20
7700	200	-150	-30	20

7800	400	−250	−130	20
7900	600	−350	−230	20
8000	800	−450	−330	20

Buy 2 ATM Calls

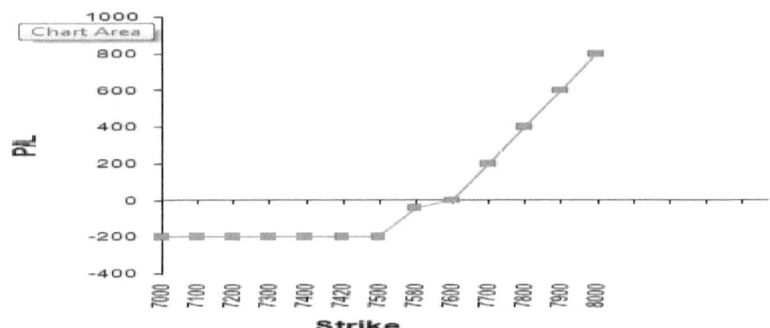

Sell 1 ITM Call

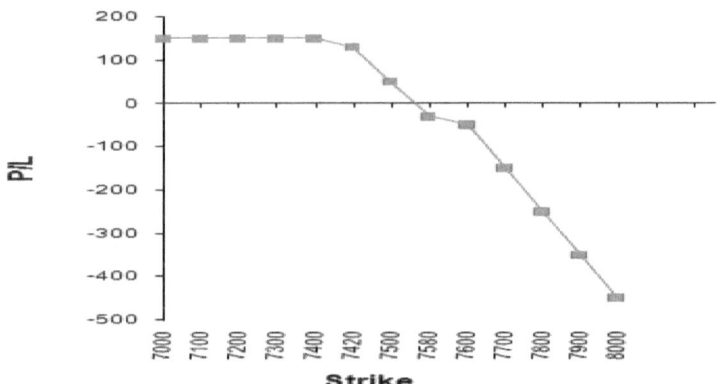

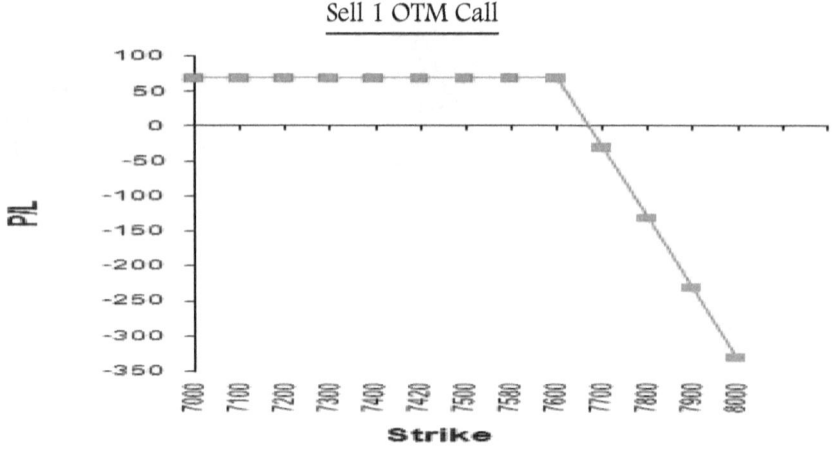

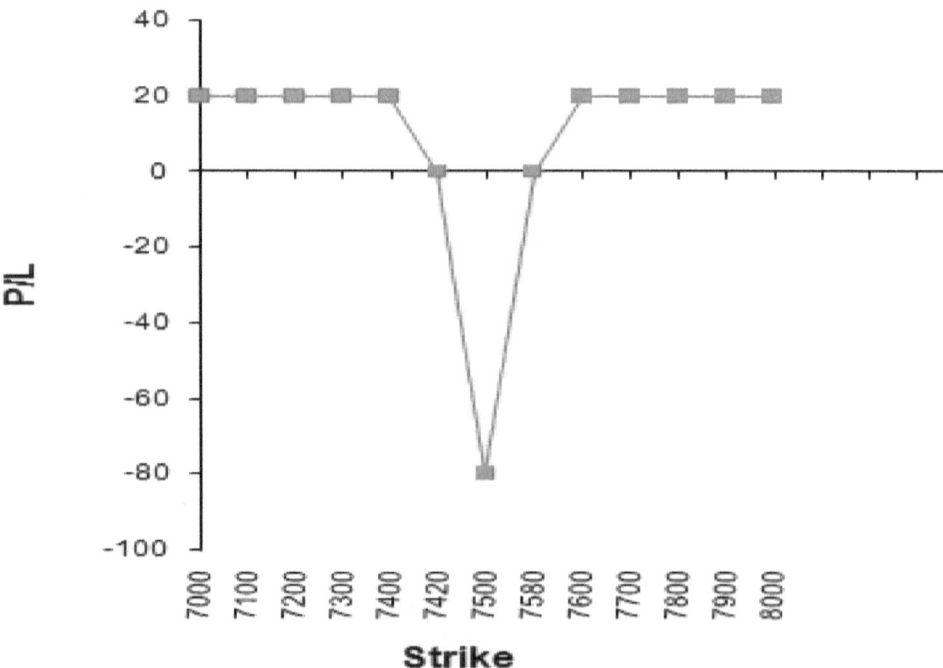

104

STRATEGY 21: LONG CALL CONDOR: BUY 1 ITM CALL OPTION (LOWER STRIKE), SELL 1 ITM CALL OPTION (LOWER MIDDLE), SELL 1 OTM CALL OPTION (HIGHER MIDDLE) AND BUY 1 OTM CALL OPTION (HIGHER STRIKE)

The strategy is suitable when the underlying is in range bound. A long call condor strategy is very similar to long butterfly strategy. The only difference is that the two middle sold options have different strikes. The strategy is constructed by buying 1 ITM call option (lower strike), selling 1 ITM call option (lower middle), selling 1 OTM call option (higher middle) and buying 1 OTM call option (higher strike). The strategy shows the maximum profit when underlying remains range bound and shows very less volatility i.e. the underlying expires at the middle strike. The long call positions at the outside strikes eliminate the risk and the risk is capped on both the sides.

Example- Ms. Pooja expects nifty to be less volatile and remains range bound. When nifty was trading at 8000 she decides to enter in to a long call condor strategy by buying 1 ITM call option with a strike price of 7800 at a premium of Rs.240, sells 1 ITM call option with a strike price of 7900 at a premium of Rs.120, sells 1 OTM call option with a strike price of Rs. 8100 at premium of Rs. 40 and buys 1 OTM call option with a strike price of 8200 at a premium of Rs.20. The net debit to the strategy is Rs. 100 which is also her maximum possible loss.

When to use Long Call Condor Strategy

The strategy is useful when investor expects very low volatility in underlying and that the underlying will remain range bound till the expiry.

Risk & Reward associated with this strategy

The risk & rewards are limited to the strategy. Risk is limited to the minimum of the difference between the lower strike call spread less the higher call spread less the total premium paid for the condor. The maximum profit can be realized when the underlying expires at the two middle strike prices.

Breakeven

Upper Breakeven Point = Highest Strike − Net Debit

Lower Breakeven Point = Lowest Strike + Net Debit

Strategy: Long Call Condor

(Buy 1 ITM call, Sell 1 ITM call, Sell 1 OTM call and Buy 1 OTM call option)

Nifty Index	Current Market Price	8000
Buy 1 ITM call option	Strike Price	7800
Ms. Pooja Pays	Premium	240
Sell 1 ITM call option	Strike Price	7900
Ms. Pooja receives	Premium	120
Sell 1 OTM call option	Strike Price	8100
Ms. Pooja Receives	Premium	40
Buy 1 OTM Call option	Strike price	8200
Ms. Pooja pays	Premium	20
	Break Even Point (Upper)	8100
	Break Even point (Lower)	7900

The Payoff Schedule

Nifty Closes at (Rs.) on expiry	Net Payoff from 1 ITM Call Bought (Rs.)	Net Payoff from 1 ITM Call Sold (Rs.)	Net Payoff from 1 OTM Call Sold (Rs.)	Net payoff from 1 OTM Call Bought (Rs.)	Net payoff from Strategy(Rs.)
7500	-240	120	40	-20	-100
7600	-240	120	40	-20	-100
7700	-240	120	40	-20	-100
7800	-240	120	40	-20	-100
7900	-140	120	40	-20	0
8000	0	20	40	-20	40
8100	60	-80	40	-20	0
8200	160	-180	-60	-20	-100
8300	260	-280	-160	80	-100
8400	360	-380	-260	180	-100
8500	460	-480	-360	280	-100
8600	560	-580	-460	380	-100
8700	660	-680	-560	480	-100

Buy 1 ITM Call option (Lower Strike)

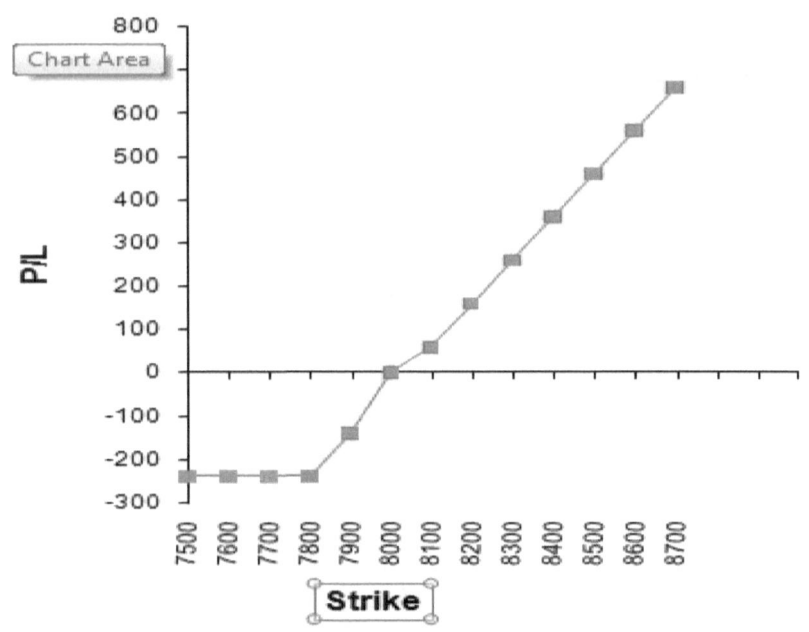

Sell 1 ITM Call (Lower Middle)

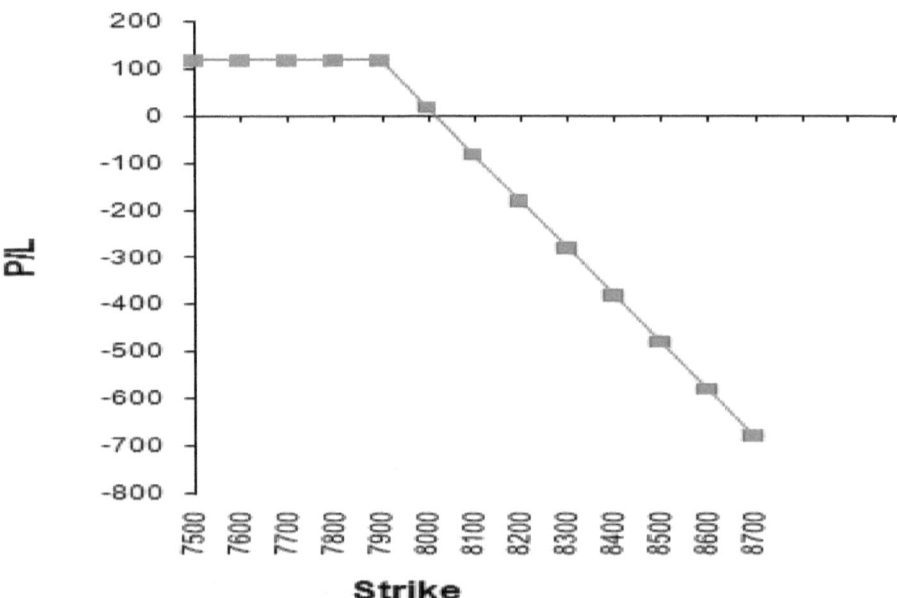

Sell 1 OTM Call Option (Higher Middle)

Buy 1 OTM call option (Higher Strike)

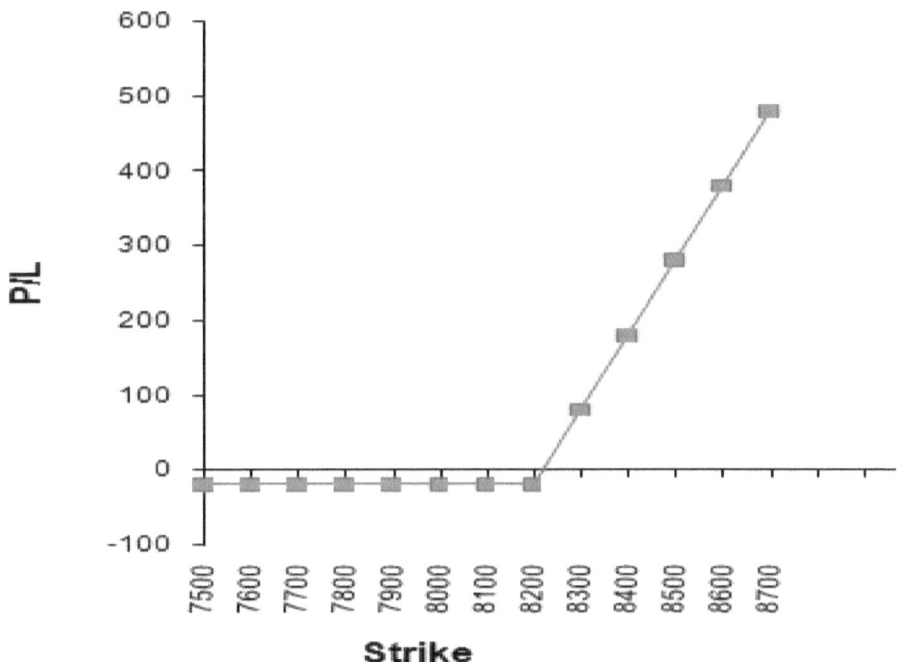

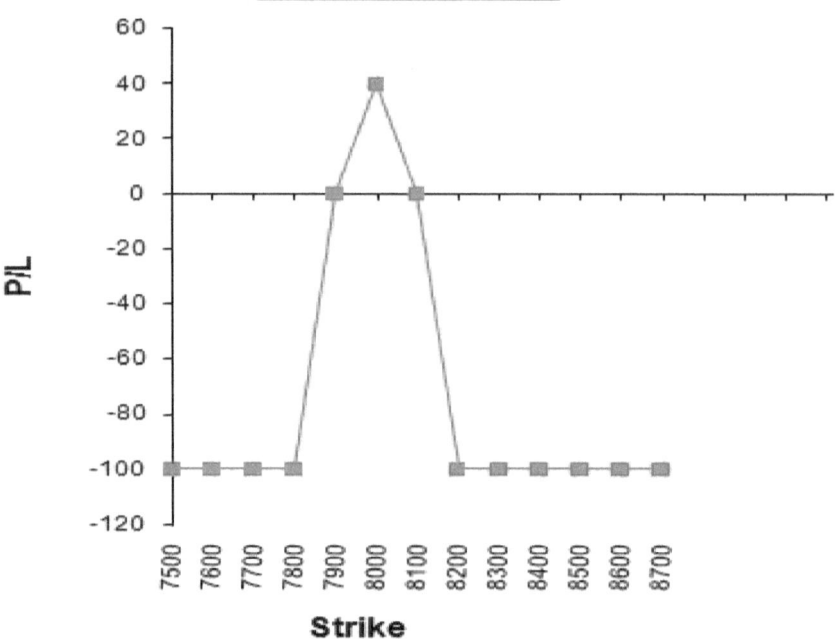

STRATEGY 22: SHORT CALL CONDOR: SHORT 1 ITM CALL OPTION (LOWER STRIKE), LONG 1 ITM CALL OPTION (LOWER MIDDLE), LONG 1 OTM CALL OPTION (HIGHER MIDDLE) AND SHORT 1 OTM CALL OPTION (HIGHER STRIKE)

The strategy is suitable when the underlying is volatile and investor expects a big move. A short call condor strategy is very similar to a short butterfly strategy. The strategy is constructed by selling 1 ITM call (lower strike), buying 1 ITM call option (lower middle), buying 1 OTM call option (higher middle) and selling 1 OTM call option (higher strike).the strategy shows the maximum profit when underlying stock/index finishes on either side of the upper or lower strike prices at expiration.

Example- Ms. Ziva Expects nifty to be more volatile and can show a big move. Nifty was trading at 8500 level and she decides to enter short call condor strategy by selling 1 ITM call option of strike price of 8300 at a premium of Rs.40, buys 1 ITM call option of 8400 at a premium of Rs.25, buys 1 OTM call option of strike price of 8600 at a premium of Rs.10 and sells 1 OTM call option of 8700 at a premium of Rs. 5. The net credit to the strategy is Rs.10.

When to use Long Call Condor Strategy

The strategy is useful when investor expects very high volatility in underlying and that the underlying can show a big move in either direction.

Risk & Reward associated with this strategy

The risk & rewards are limited to the strategy. The maximum loss of short call condor strategy occurs at the center of the option spread. The maximum profit occurs when the underlying breaks the upper or lower strike prices.

Breakeven

Upper Breakeven Point = Highest Strike – Net Credit
Lower Breakeven Point = Lowest Strike + Net Credit

Strategy: Short Call Condor

(Buy 1 ITM call, Sell 1 ITM call, Sell 1 OTM call and Buy 1 OTM call option)

Nifty Index	Current Market Price	8500
Sell 1 ITM call option	Strike Price	8300
Ms. Ziva Receives	Premium	40
Buy1 ITM call option	Strike Price	8400
Ms. Ziva Pays	Premium	25
Buy 1 OTM call option	Strike Price	8600
Ms. Ziva Pays	Premium	10
Sell 1 OTM Call option	Strike price	8700
Ms. Ziva Receives	Premium	5
	Break Even Point (Upper)(8700-10)	8690
	Break Even point (Lower)(8300+10)	8310

The Payoff Schedule

Nifty Closes at (Rs.) on expiry	Net Payoff from 1 ITM Call Sold (Rs.)	Net Payoff from 1 ITM Call Bought (Rs.)	Net Payoff from 1 OTM Call Bought (Rs.)	Net payoff from 1 OTM Call Sold (Rs.)	Net payoff from Strategy (Rs.)
8000	40	-25	-10	5	10
8100	40	-25	-10	5	10
8200	40	-25	-10	5	10
8300	40	-25	-10	5	10
8310	30	-25	-10	5	0

8400	-60	-25	-10	5	-90
8500	-160	75	-10	5	-90
8600	-260	175	-10	5	-90
8690	-350	265	80	5	0
8700	-360	275	90	5	10
8800	-460	375	190	-95	10
9000	-560	475	290	-195	10

Short 1 ITM Call option (Lower strike)

Long 1 ITM Call Option (Lower Middle)

Long 1 OTM Call Option (Higher Middle)

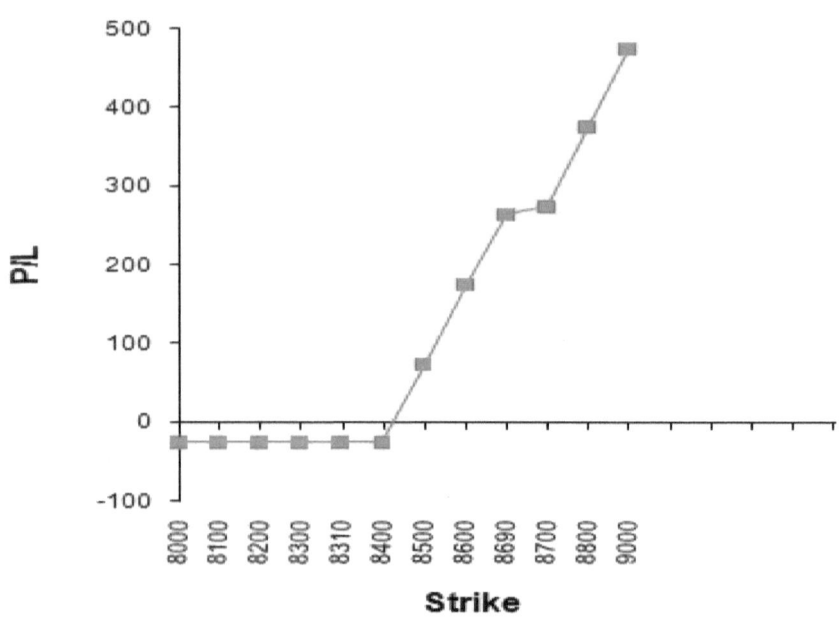

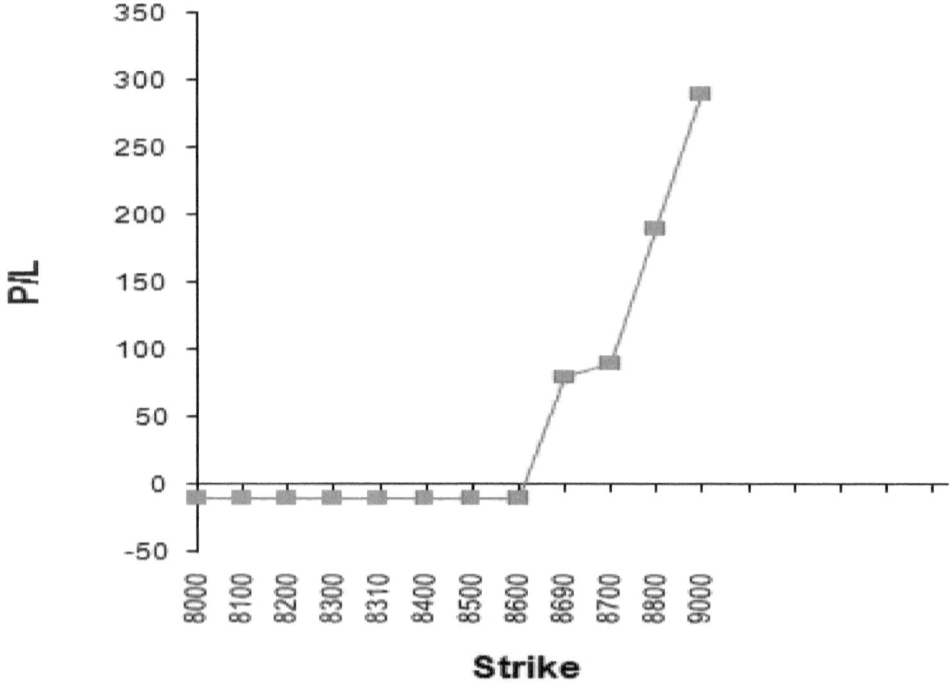

Short 1 OTM Call Option (Higher Strike)

Short Call Condor Strategy

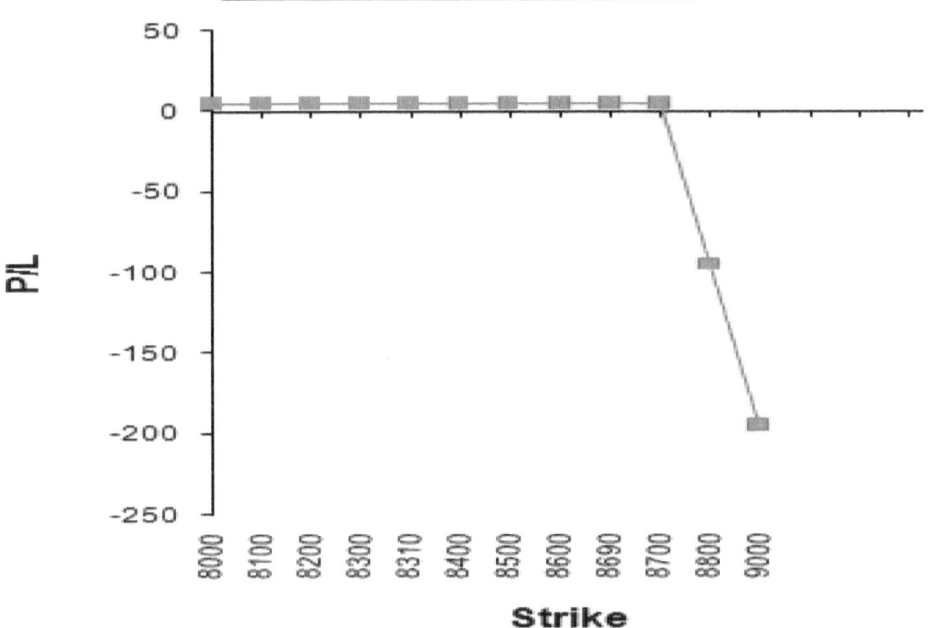

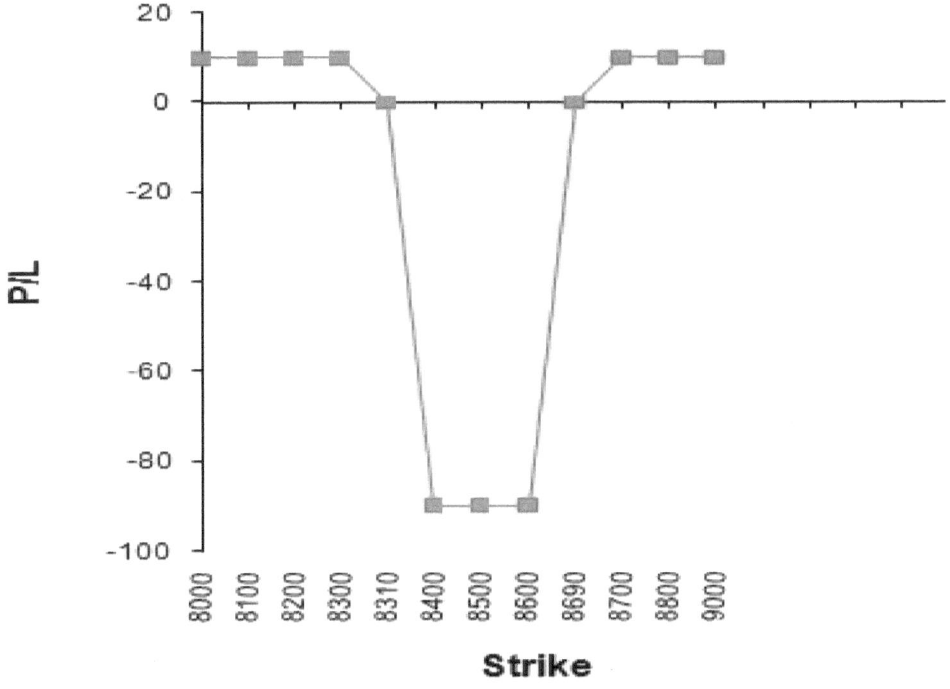

Option Greeks

To understand Option Greeks, one must know the variables of the options. There are five variables which affects the premium of the options. Change in these variables will change the price of options. These variables are:

1) Spot Price.

2) Strike price.

3) Time to maturity.

4) Volatility.

5) Rate of interest.

These five factors make the option premium. Change in any one or all variables will lead to change in option price. If price of the option changes it means one of these variables is surely impacted which results in change in the price of option. At least one of the variables must change to change the option price.

So the question is if any of the variables changes than what will be the effect of that on the option premium? How much option premium will change by change in the variables? And this is why option Greeks comes in to the picture. Option Greeks helps us to know how much option premium will change if there is a change in any of the option variables.

There are five option Greeks which tells us how much option premium will change due to change in the option variables. Below are the Option Greeks –
A) Delta
B) Gamma
C) Theta
D) Vega
E) Rho

DELTA

Delta tells us how much option premium will move for a 1 Rupee change in underlying? i.e. if the underlying asset changes by Rs.1 then its option (call or put) will change by how much?

Though we know that the price of the option is derived from the underlying asset but the options does not move exactly the same as underlying. And this is where the delta helps us to know the theoretical movement in option based on the movement of underlying. The delta of the option can be between -1 to +1. Let's say if the delta of the option is +1 then the option premium will change by Rs.1 for every one rupee change in underlying. If the underlying increases by one rupee then its call option (positive delta) will increase by one and put option (negative delta) will decrease by one. If the underlying decreases by one then its call option premium will decrease by one and put option will increase by one.

Let's say if the underlying is increases by one and its option is only increased by 0.5, it means its delta is 0.5. For every single move in underlying its option premium will move by 0.5 only.

Delta= Change in option price/ change in underlying

Delta is denoted by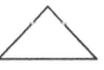

Characteristics of Delta

- Delta is positive for call option and negative for put option (long positions in both).

- Delta ranges between −1 and +1. As the option price is derived from the underlying, the option cannot have delta more than the asset. Asset has the highest delta.

- Delta for in-the-money call option is 1.

- Delta for in-the-money put option is −1.

- Delta for at-the-money is around 0.5 or −0.5. It depends on options type i.e. call or put. At-the-money-call option delta is 0.5 and at-the-money-put option delta is −0.5.

- Delta for out-of-the-money option is 0.

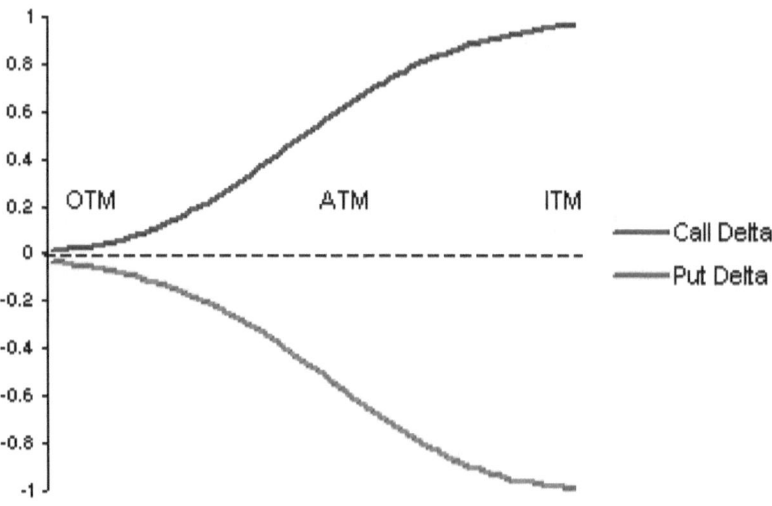

Delta also acts as a probability indicator for underlying expiry. It tells us what's the probability that option will expire in-the-money. If the delta of a Nifty call option of 7000 strike price is 0.40, it means there is a 40% probability that nifty will end above

7000 on expiry, which also means that there is a 60% probability that nifty may end below 7000 on expiry. It also tells us that the nifty 7000 put option delta must be -0.60 if its call has delta of 0.40.

So next time when buying Deep-out-of-money options please look at its delta and see if it's worth buying a cheap option/deep-out-of-money option which are having low deltas like 0.08/0.10 which states that if you will take the trade 100 times you are going to make money only 8 to 10 times and are going to lose money for remaining 90 times.

Gamma

Gamma tells us how much option delta will move for a 1 Rupee change in underlying? i.e. if underlying changes by 1 then option delta will change by how much? Gamma helps in measuring the rate of change in delta with respect to change in underlying price.

Like Delta, change in Gamma is constant with every change in underlying. Gamma for option decreases as the option goes deep into or out of the money. Generally the gamma is higher when the underlying price is near the strike price of the option. The deep in-the-money or out-of-the-money options have Gamma values close to zero.

<u>Gamma</u>- It is the rate of change of delta.

Example- let's say ABC ltd is trading at Rs.100 and its call option with strike price of Rs.100 is trading at Rs. 8 and it has a delta of 0.5 means for every change in underlying its option price will change by Rs 0.50. Now the option will be trading at Rs.8.5 when underlying reaches to Rs.101. But this is not the case that will happen every time and the option will not move every time with same acceleration. As the option goes in the or out of the money the acceleration factor delta for the option changes. When stock moves from Rs.101 to Rs.102 lets say the call option moves from 8.5 to 9.10 it means now the option has move of 0.60 (0.10 increase in delta also known as Gamma). It means now the Gamma is 0.10 and the delta will be adjusted to 0.6 from 0.5 and the option will move 0.6 for every move in underlying.

However, if the underlying falls by Rs.1 then the delta of the option will decrease by 10% to 0.4.

Theta

Theta tells us how much value of option will erode with the passage of time. This is called as time decay in the option price. As the one trading day passes and the expiration day comes nearer the option loses its value and this value is referred as time value of the option.

Theta is the rate of change of option price with respect to passage of time. It measures how much option will lose (due to time value) if all other factors remain constant and a one trading day passes and time to expiration approaches.

Example- An investor bought a Nifty option of strike price of 8000 at Rs. 50 when nifty is trading at 8030 and time to expiration is 10 days. Here the intrinsic value of option is Rs.30 and time value is Rs.20. If the theta of the option is Rs.2 then the option will lose Rs.2 every day if all other factor remains equal. If other things remain equal the option will be at Rs.40 after 5 days and this loss in option value is known as time decay of option. As the expiration day comes nearer the option will reach to its intrinsic value.

At-the-money options have higher theta as compared to in-the-money and out-of-the-money options. Longer term options have zero theta because they do not lose value on daily basis. Shorter term options have more theta than longer term options. Theta of the options increases as the time to expiration approaches. Time decay is at its peak when the expiration is nearer.

Longer term options have higher time value but the time decay (loss in value of option) is higher to shorter term options and whose expiration is nearer. The reason of having more time value to longer term option is that buyer of the option has more time for successful outcome and seller charges higher premium for this increased risk of uncertainty.

All options have only intrinsic value at the expiration and the time value erodes each and every day. Theta helps in finding how much of the time value will erode as each day passes.

Theta is negative for buyer of the options and positive for seller of the options. Theta is negative for option buyer because as the time passes the options losses its time value and is positive for option seller because seller gains (when Short on options) as the option is losing its value.

Vega

Vega is the rate of change of the option price with respect to change in the volatility. It measures the sensitivity (price change) of the options with respect to the changes in the volatility of the underlying asset. Volatility is the amount and speed at which prices moves up and down.

Vega helps in determining the change in option price in reaction to 1% change in the volatility. Vega tells us how much option price will change when there is an increase or decrease in volatility of the underlying asset. The underlying asset has zero Vega, only the option price will change with respect to change in volatility. Change in volatility does not affect underlying asset and future prices.

Vega is positive for long positions in both calls and puts, and negative for short positions. The long position in options will increase in value if the volatility increases and decrease in option value when volatility decreases.

Vega is largest for at-the-money options and declines for both in-the-money and out-of-money options.

Example- If SBI is trading at Rs.260 and the call option of 260 strike price is trading at Rs.3 and the Vega is 0.30, then a 1% change in volatility will lead to option price to Rs.3.30. If the volatility declines than the option price will fall to Rs.2.70. Here, Vega is 0.30 which indicates that the option will move by 0.30 in value with respect to 1% change in Volatility.

Rho

$$\rho$$

Rho tells us how much option price should change with respect to 1% change in interest rates. Interest rates here refer to Risk free rate of interest.

Risk-free rate represents the interest that an investor would expect from an absolutely risk-free investment over a given period of time.

A government bond may be referred as a risk free bond as it is issued by a government agency whose risk of default is as low as negligible.

Example- If the Rho of a call option is 0.20 and call option is trading at Rs.4 and the risk free rate rises by 1% (Bond rates from 8% to 9%) then the price of call option will increase to Rs.4.20. Rho 0.20 represents that a 1% change in interest rates will change the value of option price by Rs.0.20.

As the interest rates change gradually the impact of Rho is not huge in day to day options trading.

Lambda

λ

Lambda is not exactly an option Greek but it is an important factor while measuring the leverage of a position and your portfolio as a whole. Higher the leverage, the risk will be more and also potential reward. Option leverage or Lambda can be calculated as follows-

$$\lambda = \frac{\Delta \cdot \text{Stock Price}}{\text{Option Price}}$$

The premium for options goes on decreasing as you go from in the money to out of the money options. As it decreases the cost of the option because out of the money options are much cheaper than in the money options but it also decreases the probability of your option coming in the money and increases the probability of your option expiring worthless. When you are paying lesser and lesser amount for out of the money options for controlling the same number of shares, here you are creating a greater leverage.

For example- SBI is trading at Rs. 300 and its call option of 320 strike price is trading at Rs. 6 and the days to expiration is about 5 days or a week, so its delta is low around 0.20. This means that it has only 20% probability that this strike will become in the money. So our leverage in this case will be more-

$$\lambda = \frac{0.20 \cdot 300}{6}$$

$$\lambda = 10$$

In the same manner if we have bought option of strike price of Rs. 310 which is trading at Rs.30 and whose delta is 0.60 which means it has 60% probability that this option can become in the money or the stock can hit this strike price. In this case our leverage will be low-

$$\lambda = \frac{0.60 \cdot 300}{30}$$

$\lambda = 6$

Next time when you are paying lesser for any out of the money options for controlling the same number of shares, do focus on the leverage (λ) and its probability (Δ) of becoming in the money option.

Notes

www.ingramcontent.com/pod-product-compliance
Lightning Source LLC
Chambersburg PA
CBHW031428210526
45464CB00005B/2105